D1610054

1980s Project Studies/Council on Foreign Relations

STUDIES AVAILABLE

NUCLEAR PROLIFERATION:
Motivations, Capabilities, and Strategies for Control
Studies by Ted Greenwood and by Harold A. Feiveson and
Theodore B. Taylor

ALTERNATIVES TO MONETARY DISORDER
Studies by Fred Hirsch and Michael Doyle and by Edward L. Morse

CHINA'S FUTURE:
Foreign Policy and Economic Development in the Post-Mao Era
Studies by Allen S. Whiting and by Robert F. Dernberger

INTERNATIONAL DISASTER RELIEF:
Toward a Responsive System
Stephen Green

STUDIES FORTHCOMING

Some 25 additional volumes of the 1980s Project work will be appearing in the course of the next year or two. Most will contain independent but related studies concerning issues of potentially great importance in the next decade and beyond, such as the control of strategic weaponry, resource management, terrorism, relations between the developing and developed societies, and the world market in conventional arms, among many others. Additionally, a number of volumes will be devoted to particular regions of the world, concentrating especially on political and economic development trends outside the industrialized West.

Nuclear Proliferation

MOTIVATIONS, CAPABILITIES, AND STRATEGIES FOR CONTROL

TED GREENWOOD

HAROLD A. FEIVESON

THEODORE B. TAYLOR

Introduction by David C. Gompert

1980s Project/Council on Foreign Relations

McGRAW-HILL BOOK COMPANY

New York   St. Louis   San Francisco
Auckland   Bogotá   Düsseldorf   Johannesburg   London   Madrid
Mexico   Montreal   New Delhi   Panama   Paris   São Paulo
Singapore   Sydney   Tokyo   Toronto

The Council on Foreign Relations, Inc., is a nonprofit and nonpartisan organization devoted to promoting improved understanding of international affairs through the free exchange of ideas. Its membership of about 1,700 persons throughout the United States is made up of individuals with special interest and experience in international affairs. The Council has no affiliation with and receives no funding from the United States government.

The Council publishes the quarterly journal *Foreign Affairs* and, from time to time, books and monographs that in the judgment of the Council's Committee on Studies are responsible treatments of significant international topics worthy of presentation to the public. The 1980s Project is a research effort of the Council; as such, 1980s Project Studies have been similarly reviewed through procedures of the Committee on Studies. As in the case of all Council publications, statements of fact and expressions of opinion contained in 1980s Project Studies are the sole responsibility of their authors.

The editor of this book was Michael Schwarz for the Council on Foreign Relations. Thomas Quinn and Michael Hennelly were the editors for McGraw-Hill Book Company. Christopher Simon was the designer and Milton J. Heiberg supervised the production. This book was set in Times Roman by Creative Book Services, Inc.

Printed and bound by R. R. Donnelley & Sons.

Library of Congress Cataloging in Publication Data

Greenwood, Ted
Nuclear proliferation.

(1980s project/Council on Foreign Relations)
Bibliography: p.
Includes index.
1. Atomic weapons and disarmament.   I.   Feiveson,
Harold A., joint author.   II.   Taylor, Theodore B.,
joint author.   III.   Title.   IV.   Series:
Council on Foreign Relations.   1980s project/Council
on Foreign Relations.
JX1974.7.G74   327'.174   76-30588
ISBN 0-07-024344-1
ISBN 0-07-024345-X pbk.
1 2 3 4 5 6 7 8 9 RRDRRD 7 0 9 8 7

Contents

Foreword: The 1980s Project

The essays in this volume, offering long-term proposals for dealing with the problem of nuclear proliferation, are part of a stream of studies to be produced in the course of the 1980s Project of the Council on Foreign Relations. Each 1980s Project study analyzes an issue that is likely to be of international concern during the coming decade or two.

The ambitious purpose of the 1980s Project is to examine important political and economic problems not only individually but in relationship to one another. Some studies or books produced by the Project will primarily emphasize the interrelationship of issues. In the case of other, more specifically focused studies, a considerable effort has been made to write, review, and criticize them in the context of more general Project work. Each Project study is thus capable of standing on its own; at the same time it has been shaped by a broader perspective.

The 1980s Project had its origins in the widely held recognition that many of the assumptions, policies, and institutions that have characterized international relations during the past 30 years are inadequate to the demands of today and the foreseeable demands of the period between now and 1990 or so. Over the course of the next decade, substantial adaptation of institutions and behavior will be needed to respond to the changed circumstances of the 1980s and beyond. The Project seeks to identify those future conditions and the kinds of adaptation they might require. It is not the Project's purpose to arrive at a single or exclusive set of goals. Nor does it focus upon the foreign policy or national interests of the United States alone. Instead, it seeks to identify goals that are compatible with the perceived interests of most states, despite differences in ideology and in level of economic development.

The published products of the Project are aimed at a broad readership —including policy makers, potential policy makers, and those who would influence the policy-making process—but are confined to no single nation or region. The authors of Project studies were therefore asked to remain mindful of interests broader than those of any one society and to take fully into account the likely realities of domestic politics in the principal societies involved. All those who have worked in the

Project, however, have tried not to be captives of the status quo; they have sought to question the inevitability of existing patterns of thought and behavior that restrain desirable change and to look for ways in which those patterns might in time be altered or their consequences mitigated.

The 1980s Project is at once a series of separate attacks upon a number of urgent and potentially urgent international problems and also a collective effort, involving a substantial number of persons in the United States and abroad, to bring those separate approaches to bear upon one another and to suggest the kinds of choices that might be made among them. The Project involves more than 300 participants. A small central staff and a steering Coordinating Group have worked to define the questions and to assess the compatibility of policy prescriptions. Nearly 100 authors, from more than a dozen countries, have been at work on separate studies. Ten working groups of specialists and generalists have been convened to subject the Project's studies to critical scrutiny and to help in the process of identifying interrelationships among them.

The 1980s Project is the largest single research and studies effort the Council on Foreign Relations has undertaken in its 55-year history, comparable in conception only to a major study of the postwar world, the War and Peace Studies, undertaken by the Council during the Second World War. At that time, the impetus to the effort was the discontinuity caused by worldwide conflict and visible and inescapable need to rethink, replace, and supplement many of the features of the international system that had prevailed before the war. The discontinuities in today's world are less obvious and, even when occasionally quite visible—as in the abandonment of gold convertibility and fixed monetary parities—only briefly command the spotlight of public attention. That new institutions and patterns of behavior are needed in many areas is widely acknowledged, but the sense of need is less urgent: existing institutions have not for the most part dramatically failed and collapsed. The tendency, therefore, is to make do with outmoded arrangements and to improvise rather than to undertake a basic analysis of the problems that lie before us and of the demands that those problems will place upon all nations.

The 1980s Project is based upon the belief that serious effort and integrated forethought can contribute—indeed, are indispensable—to progress in the next decade toward a more humane, peaceful, productive, and just world. And it rests upon the hope that participants in its deliberations and readers of Project publications—whether or not they agree with an author's point of view—may be helped to think more informedly about the opportunities and the dangers that lie ahead and the consequences of various possible courses of future action.

The 1980s Project has been made possible by generous grants from the Ford Foundation, the Lilly Endowment, the Andrew W. Mellon Foundation, the Rockefeller Foundation, and the German Marshall Fund of the United States. Neither the Council on Foreign Relations nor any of those foundations is responsible for statements of fact and expressions of opinion contained in publications of the 1980s Project; they are the sole responsibility of the individual authors under whose names they appear. But the Council on Foreign Relations and the staff of the 1980s Project take great pleasure in placing those publications before a wide readership both in the United States and abroad.

Richard H. Ullman
Director, the 1980s Project

During 1975 and 1976, ten Working Groups met to explore major international issues and to subject initial drafts of 1980s Project studies to critical review. Those who chaired Project Working Groups were:

Cyrus R. Vance, Working Group on Nuclear Weapons and Other Weapons of Mass Destruction

Leslie H. Gelb, Working Group on Armed Conflict

Roger Fisher, Working Group on Transnational Violence and Subversion

Rev. Theodore M. Hesburgh, Working Group on Human Rights

Joseph S. Nye, Jr., Working Group on the Political Economy of North-South Relations

Harold Van B. Cleveland, Working Group on Macroeconomic Policies and International Monetary Relations

Lawrence C. McQuade, Working Group on Principles of International Trade

William Diebold, Jr., Working Group on Multinational Enterprises

Eugene B. Skolnikoff, Working Group on the Environment, the Global Commons, and Economic Growth

Miriam Camps, Working Group on Industrial Policy

The members of the 1980s Project staff are:

Miriam Camps	*Catherine Gwin*
William Diebold, Jr.	*Roger Hansen*
David Gompert	*Edward L. Morse*

Richard H. Ullman (Director)

The Committee on Studies of the Board of Directors of the Council on Foreign Relations was the governing body of the 1980s Project. The Committee's members as of December 31, 1976, were:

The Coordinating Group of the 1980s Project had a central advisory role in the work of the Project. Its members as of December 31, 1976, were:

Introduction: Nuclear Proliferation and the 1980s Project

David C. Gompert

Nuclear proliferation raises certain fundamental normative issues that no amount of theorizing can erase. To arrest the spread of nuclear weapons would be to perpetuate an international status quo in which some societies are denied political and strategic assets that other societies, certainly no more deserving, are entitled to have. Yet to condone nuclear proliferation in the interest of reducing the inegalitarian nature of the international system would be to abdicate responsibility for minimizing the risk of nuclear conflict. Pretending that greater equality among states and nuclear safety are fully compatible values might lead to the achievement of neither. But pursuing either value while wholly ignoring the other would be equally futile in the long run: equality cannot survive in a dangerous world, and safety will be transitory unless rooted in at least the credible promise of greater equality. Dealing with proliferation means confronting this dilemma.

Scholars and practitioners alike habitually isolate issues to facilitate comprehension. But proliferation can be neither adequately understood nor effectively dealt with as a discrete problem. The integral relationship of nuclear proliferation with other important international questions cannot be suspended for the sake of academic clarity. Proliferation is the intersection of a number of important issues and trends, no one of which will decide how events will unfold:

- Growing energy demand both in the industrialized and in the oil-poor developing countries is intensifying interest in expanding fission power generation and, particularly, interest in future reliance on

1

nuclear regenerative processes based on plutonium. As these technologies spread, so also do the materials, facilities, and skills that are used to manufacture nuclear weapons. Despite serious concerns in some countries about the safety and ecological effects of nuclear power, the commitment to expand this energy source continues to develop momentum, if not in the United States, certainly in scores of other countries. To retard this development in the interest of curbir.g nuclear proliferation could mean even greater dependence on imported petroleum, at least through the 1980s, than has already been experienced, especially if other sources of energy, such as coal, are not rapidly developed.

- The questionable credibility of the American strategic nuclear umbrella for purposes other than to deter nuclear attack against the United States is causing a number of formerly satisfied allies to consider investing in their own nuclear security. Yet restoring full confidence in American nuclear protection could require a more robust United States strategic posture than one might prefer. For instance, the preference expressed by many for the withdrawal of American nuclear weapons positioned abroad must be weighed against the danger that such a measure might encourage proliferation. Perhaps more critical, growing doubts about the credibility of American commitments to help—by intervening, if necessary—in the defense of traditional allies may increase the likelihood of their turning to nuclear weapons for security against conventional threats. Yet the price of forestalling such tendencies by maintaining American readiness to intervene is high, if not prohibitive. Since Moscow's clients are not comparably dependent on the Soviet Union for their protection, the weakening of security ties in the East probably would not stimulate proliferation (except perhaps by North Korea).

- The availability of sophisticated conventional weaponry may make the acquisition of nuclear weapons appear less important to those potential proliferants who are motivated primarily by regional security concerns. New developments in weapons technology may make widely accessible conventional systems at least as effective as nuclear weapons in meeting defense needs of most states. While such weapons may not deter potential aggressors as reliably as nuclear

2

weapons, the compunction against actually using them in military defense would be far less. At the same time, however, providing such weapons in the interest of slowing nuclear proliferation could have the opposite effect: a regime that has acquired a prodigious conventional capability—and, by the late 1980s, perhaps considerable independence from outside suppliers—might then decide that it needed only a nuclear weapons capability to qualify as a world-class military power; and much of the technology that makes the new conventional weapons so attractive—accuracy, range, reliability—is ideally suited to provide modern delivery systems for nuclear warheads. Indeed—and somewhat ironically—the fear of facilitating proliferation by providing conventional systems that can be adapted to nuclear capabilities may provide an important incentive for restraining exports of non-nuclear arms.

- The danger of nuclear proliferation is sometimes seen as a force that the developing world could employ, at least implicitly, to excite the industrialized societies into more equitable patterns of economic distribution and to gain representation in the high chambers of world politics where the nuclear states sit. Analysts differ as to the likelihood of such scenarios. Regardless of the actual motivation behind future proliferation decisions by Third World governments, the rhetorical justification that they are contributing to the aggregate power of the developing world is likely to evoke widespread sympathy and endorsement among other developing countries. Collective efforts by the key industrial nuclear exporters to impede proliferation would be certain to accentuate the distributional aspect of the issue.

- The question of how the international market in nuclear technology should be managed may be a continuing source of friction and suspicion among leading Western countries. Many Americans regard the French and the Germans as irresponsible in making available facilities for reprocessing spent nuclear reactor fuel, making it reusable not only in power generation but also for nuclear explosives. Meanwhile, the French and Germans suspect the United States of wanting to minimize competition with American reactor sales abroad by abolishing trade in reprocessing facilities, which other exporters offer to enhance their competitiveness. Ironically, this same set of

3

issues has stirred a cautious but clear Soviet interest in cooperation with the Western exporters to fashion a common restrictive stance on nuclear exports.

Cutting across practically all of these questions is the changing structure of the international system itself: the fragmentation and diffusion of power, of which proliferation must be seen as both a symptom and a cause. Moreover, as emerging regional powers pull away from—or are cast out of—their traditional orbits around the superpowers, it might become increasingly difficult to harmonize their nuclear postures and policies with the relatively stable East-West nuclear system. Deterrence relationships are likely to become increasingly confused and ambiguous. As security relationships become less rigid, as hierarchy erodes, former client states will enjoy greater freedom of action. And the powerful, fearing the risks of close association with new nuclear states over whom their influence is waning, may forfeit their remaining ability to restrain by terminating the old security relationships. Proliferants may find themselves more independent than they would choose to be, alone with their primitive nuclear capabilities to fend for themselves.

The lasting achievement of nonproliferation objectives must rely on more than the ad hoc manipulation of inducements and inhibitions. The legitimacy, durability, and consistency of whatever norms are to be adopted will require institutional arrangements, be they global or subglobal, technical or politicized, hierarchical or egalitarian. Whether efforts to institutionalize desirable behavior regarding the distribution of nuclear weapons should be organized specifically and exclusively for that function—or in the context of international energy institutions, general arms control institutions, or, indeed, central political institutions—is an open and perhaps crucial question.

It is one thing to recognize the need for institutions and quite another to believe that institutions will resolve the problem of proliferation. Designing international agencies and enshrining platitudes about how states ought to behave will not provide the means to avoid the dilemmas and contradictions embodied in the issue of proliferation.

THE SCOPE AND THRUST OF THIS VOLUME

In organizing the work of the 1980s Project on nuclear proliferation, the Project staff elected to split the issue and analyze each of two aspects quite independently of the other. Ted Greenwood was asked to consider primarily the question of motivations; Theodore Taylor and Harold Feiveson, that of capabilities. This explicit separation distinguishes this volume from most current writing on proliferation. We reasoned that a systematic analysis of the incentives and disincentives would be more successful if unencumbered by considerations of technical capabilities. Thus Greenwood has developed a set of prescriptions that, in his judgment, would reduce incentives at tolerable costs in terms of other international goals and values. We further reasoned that the best way to determine the degree to which technical measures alone might reduce the problem would be to suspend the question of motivations and focus on capabilities. Taylor and Feiveson have outlined the technical characteristics of a nuclear economy that they believe would be less conducive to proliferation than the one that is now gathering momentum.

It will surprise no one that Greenwood has not produced a compelling answer to the conundrum of how to induce states not to want what others hold so dearly. In his view, the rate of proliferation is a more critical question than that of whether or not the circle of states possessing nuclear weapons grows. His proposals are therefore primarily directed toward keeping the rate sufficiently slow that the necessary accommodations can be made to preserve stability. He examines a broad range of measures of conceivable value in making nuclear weapons a less attractive means of enhancing national prestige and ensuring security. He is careful to assess the drawbacks of a number of schemes, discarding many as likely to be impractical, inconsequential, or even counterproductive. His "strategy" is not an explicit call to action, but rather a compendium of ideas as to what conditons and developments would tend to inhibit proliferation. The alarmed and impatient will be troubled that Greenwood is suggesting a series of reorientations instead of a crusade.

Many analysts (Greenwood included) would regard any effort to design a "technical fix" to nuclear proliferation as tilting at windmills. By 1990 any of a score or so of states intent upon producing fission weapons will find it feasible to do so under almost any conceivable international safeguards scheme. Many will certainly be able simply to construct a reactor for the purpose of producing plutonium and a facility in which to reprocess that plutonium for nuclear weapons. Some may be able to take advantage of new uranium enrichment technologies—such as the use of lasers—to produce weapons-grade material directly, a capability that has in the past been beyond the means of all but the most advanced industrial states. While accepting these assumptions, Taylor and Feiveson argue that an expanding international nuclear power economy, properly designed and properly managed, need not contribute to the accumulation of facilities and material needed for the production of weapons.

To be sure, Feiveson and Taylor are not advocating further international growth of the use of fission power. Nor are they arguing that if such growth is inevitable it would be desirable to base it on regenerative ("recycle") processes rather than on the "once-through" processes that could conceivably exhaust uranium reserves in a matter of decades. What they do argue is that if nuclear power is to grow and is also to be based on regenerative processes, there may be a way to do it that is less hazardous than the way we are presently proceeding. Though their proposals certainly require further close examination, it would seem that the implementation of their alternative to present fuel-cycle and safeguards arrangements would mean that governments would find it difficult to keep the weapons option open solely by participating in the international nuclear market. Rather, governments would have to face the stark decision of whether or not to launch an indigenous program unambiguously designed to produce material for weapons.

Of course, capabilities and motivations are not mutually exclusive variables, as the authors of the following studies would be the first to recognize. The expansion of the civilian nuclear power industry, and the attendant creation of nuclear pressure-group interests within an increasing number of states, is certain to affect internal political alignments on the question of whether or not to keep open the option of a weapons program. Bureaucratic and nationalistic enthusiasm over a civilian nuclear power program tends to feed a desire for greater and greater nuclear independence: first the research reactor, then the power reactor, then the fuel reprocessing plant, ultimately an isotope enrichment capability. Those who would argue for a self-contained nuclear power industry are likely to be natural allies of those who would wish to avoid external relationships and obligations that would foreclose the weapons option.

Conversely, if the incentive to produce weapons exists, there may be a strong temptation to use the camouflage and resources of a fully developed national nuclear power industry rather than a separate program devoted solely to weapons production. Material diverted from commercial nuclear activities is inferior in explosive quality to material generated specifically for use in weapons, and commercial facilities are certainly more costly to construct and operate than those whose sole purpose is to produce explosives. But the civilian fuel-cycle route has the major advantage of permitting a state to guard its intentions and still politically exploit its quasi-nuclear status.

"Latent proliferation"—whereby numerous states simply refuse to foreclose or abjure the possibility of manufacturing weapons, while accumulating the resources and shortening the time required to do so—may be more likely and no less dangerous than a situation in which a gradually increasing number of states were to signal unequivocally their intent to develop and deploy nuclear weapons. Easy access to plutonium reprocessing technology serves to reinforce the perception among potential proliferants that they would be foolish, if not irresponsible, to commit themselves to nonacquisition in such an environment. Fears that the expansion of the nuclear power industry will make the spread of weapons inevitable contribute to national fears of being left behind, insecure and ill-equipped for politics in a proliferated world.

The technical and motivational bases of proliferation also come together insofar as the international norm against acquiring nuclear weapons is subverted by discriminatory application of nuclear power safeguards and by unequal access to nuclear technology. Paradoxically, states with nuclear weapons are considered "safe" and are therefore unfettered by international restrictions on and intrusions into their nuclear power activities. The inherent inequity of the nonproliferation norm is thus compounded by the fact that non-nuclear-weapons states are not only deprived but in fact penalized for their deprivation. As states manage to accumulate nuclear technology, deprivation becomes voluntary abstention, and the legitimacy of the behavioral norm assumes increased significance. As long as the states with nuclear weapons insist on unrestricted access to and unsafeguarded use of nuclear technology, the imposition of restrictions on others is seen as discriminatory and therefore inequitable. Thus the tighter the technical arrangements to impede proliferation, the less legitimate appears the behavioral norm embodied in the Non-Proliferation Treaty. Yet the looser the technical arrangements, the more likely it is that a number of states will hedge against the possibility of widespread proliferation by keeping open the option of developing weapons.

No attempt is made in this volume to merge the recommendations of the two studies into a single antiproliferation strategy, yet some tentative observations are possible concerning their fit. First, by eliminating many of the perceived inequities of the international safeguards system, the Taylor-Feiveson proposals would do much to strengthen the apparent legitimacy of the international nonproliferation norm, as urged by Greenwood. As well, greater international institutional control over the operation of key nuclear facilities would engender a greater sense of confidence that the expansion of the nuclear industry would not in itself provide the drive behind an inexorable process of proliferation. Perhaps more important, less reliance on plutonium within the industrial fuel cycle would blunt the perception that the development of weapons is only a short step beyond a civilian power program. Increasing the difficulty, expense, and degree of deliberate commitment required to produce weapons could reduce the temptation to do so, particularly when other states appeared similarly constrained. Finally, the political and security developments that Greenwood supports would foster an atmosphere in which the Taylor-Feiveson proposals would have a much better chance of being implemented. If new technical arrangements are to be instituted by consensus rather than coercion, the growing appeal of nuclear weapons has to be reversed and the suspicion surrounding nonproliferation motives dispelled.

In addition to his analysis of motivations, Greenwood offers some observations on how the international market in nuclear technology ought to be managed. Herein lies the principal disagreement between the authors of the two studies. Greenwood believes that effective technological hurdles to proliferation cannot be maintained and should therefore be replaced by—in effect, exchanged for—political and institutional barriers. Taylor and Feiveson hold that raising the technical hurdles would help circumscribe the political component of the problem. While the Taylor-Feiveson proposals are compatible with much of Greenwood's strategy, the prescriptions of the two papers regarding the world nuclear power industry diverge significantly.

Policy prescription is particularly difficult when one is dealing with nuclear proliferation because so many factors, so markedly different in nature, contribute to the issue—for instance, the general security policies of the United States and the Soviet Union, the plutonium recycle/breeder programs of the French and German governments, and the maneuverings of any of a number of emerging Third World regimes for greater importance in regional or global affairs. A comprehensive strategy to curb proliferation would require behavioral change across so wide and diverse a range of human endeavor that it could hardly be thought of as a plan for orchestrated action. At best, the strategy is a set of guidelines to aid—if not persuade—myriad actors in their vastly different pursuits to alter their courses as necessary to avoid aggravating the problem. Had the authors of the studies in this volume been asked only to indicate how the United States government should perform in respect of the issue of proliferation, their task would have been formidable enough. That the authors were instead encouraged to prescribe behavior for all actors capable of significantly influencing the issue obviously compounded the problem.

The analytical challenges faced by the authors would be of little interest to the reader were it not for the fact that they are representative of the substantive problems of "doing something" about proliferation. Taylor and Feiveson speak of *haphazard drift* in describing the present—and likely future—international course of nuclear power development. The term might be employed no less appropriately to depict the welter of actors and policy interests that bear on the motivational side of the issue addressed by Greenwood. In a way, it is the disjointedness of relevant policy making more than the absence of good reason or goodwill that leaves one pessimistic about the prospects of controlling proliferation. Policy observers spend much of their time decrying "concentrations of power"—usually with good cause. Particularly in the nuclear area, it is widely assumed that policy is easily manipulated by a narrow circle of like-minded bureaucrats and industrialists. But in fact it is the dispersion of policy-making authority among entrenched actors and activities and the resultant parochialism that bode continued drift and failure.

Consider just the Taylor-Feiveson prescriptions for alternatives to a plutonium economy. As the authors make clear, their ideas are highly preliminary, designed only to encourage deliberation. But even if the validity of their arguments were beyond all doubt, one could not be sanguine about an end to the haphazard drift. Indeed, it may not even be possible to brake the process long enough to permit sober consideration of alternatives, much less to effect major change. No single actor can decisively affect the international course of nuclear power. Even within the United States—clearly the most important actor—the military-industrial-nuclear-research complex is, ironically, largely unmanageable, though there are lines of authority, accountability, and coordination that would permit something approximating a course change. Yet even a sustained policy initiative on the part of a hypothetically unified American government could be disabled by the cumulative, if ostensibly unrelated, activities of, for example, French nuclear power enthusiasts, the Pakistani Defense Ministry, and the Organization of Petroleum Exporting Countries. The limits of unilateral action—by the United States or by any of the countless other actors involved with nonproliferation—engender a sense of futility and, therefore, narrow-mindedness among all.

While no one party can implement a nonproliferation strategy, a multitude of parties—chiefs of state, bureaucracies, industrial interests, electorates—can, by action or inaction, affect the future evolution of the proliferation issue. Thus the arguments in this volume—Greenwood's no less than Taylor's and Feiveson's—are directed internationally toward all those who have a relevant policy role and, perhaps more important, toward all upon whose support policymakers depend. Not all will be convinced; indeed, the interests of some might plainly not be served by what the authors propose.

OTHER PERSPECTIVES

A number of important and widely held views regarding nuclear proliferation are not really represented in this volume. Among them is the opinion that the resistance of the nuclear weapons states to meaningful strategic arms reductions is the principal obstacle to curbing proliferation. In this view, the glacial pace of strategic arms control and the growing gap, in terms of raw megatonnage, between the superpowers and all other states serve to sharpen the suspicion that the two founders of the Non-Proliferation Treaty had a totally one-sided process in mind all along. Years of negotiations over the levels and testing of strategic arms have failed to produce reductions or a comprehensive test ban. It is therefore a blatant affront to the non-nuclear states for the superpowers to moralize about the dangers of proliferation when the cargo of a single missile-bearing submarine has more destructive potential than all potential proliferants combined could amass in the next decade. Neither is the performance of the other nuclear states particularly helpful: France and China so cherish their sovereign prerogatives that they resist any international agreement that would constrain their nuclear weapons programs. Those who subscribe to this general view believe that until the nuclear weapons states stop accentuating the importance of nuclear weapons and themselves begin a process of denuclearization, there will continue to be an inexorable groundswell of interest among other states in developing weapons of their own.

A second point of view that merits attention is that (stated somewhat extremely) nuclear proliferation is so severe a problem that those with the power to impede it should undertake to do so however great the cost. Many persons of diverse political sentiments believe that the international community, as it were, is living on borrowed time and that the alternative to an intensive effort to stem proliferation is a chain of events that would culminate in cataclysm. There is no single set of prescriptions that invariably derives from this perspective, but rather a diverse assortment of dramatic proposals: a general moratorium on nuclear power—or at least all international nuclear transactions, joint Soviet-American or unilateral nuclear guarantees to states (e.g., Pakistan) with valid nuclear security concerns, or severe economic and diplomatic sanctions against states that acquire nuclear weapons. Some adherents to the more alarmed view would favor the imposition of a regime that would in effect outlaw proliferation. Where Greenwood urges restraint in trying to buy off prospective proliferants with conventional arms, those of this perspective would argue that an insecure, inadequately armed state will find nuclear weapons irresistible and will be all the more impelled to use them in the absence of conventional options. Where Taylor and Feiveson allow for continued national control of nuclear reactors, some would insist that international control of virtually all nuclear facilities is imperative. In short, those who believe that proliferation will eclipse all other international problems for the 1980s and beyond will be dissatisfied that the authors in this volume have not strayed further from accepted notions of what is feasible and have not given nonproliferation precedence over all other international goals.

A third set of perspectives centers on the belief that proliferation is neither generally nor, in most cases, specifically undesirable. Many proponents of this view would contend that the dangers of proliferation have been inflated by those whose monopolistic position as the custodians of strategic power is threatened. The diffusion of nuclear capabilities, like the diffusion of power more generally, will, in the judgment of many observers, erode the hierarchical features of the international system and help right the imbalance by which the powerful remain rich and the weak impoverished. To them, proliferation is an element in a general pattern of challenge to an unjust status quo. They regard any suggestion that the ''mature'' nuclear states are more trustworthy than the challengers as specious and self-serving, if not racist. If some members of this school are not unabashed proponents of proliferation, they are agnostics, claiming that the dissolution of blocs and concentrations of power would seem to have no less appeal than the perpetration of dependencies based on the extension of nuclear umbrellas by the two global powers. Finally, some analysts (including Greenwood, to some degree) would maintain that a world of 10 or 20 nuclear powers could be as stable as today's world provided there was enough time and enough wisdom to adapt security relationships to the shifting configurations of power.

SOME CONTEXTUAL OBSERVATIONS

The beliefs one has about the sources of proliferation and the proper way of dealing with it depend importantly on one's contextual interests and concerns. Yet proliferation is entangled with so wide a range of issues that no single analytic context is adequate. As well, a normative orientation based on a narrow vision of proliferation may ignore certain values that were not thought to be at stake but are. In the remaining pages I would like to suggest how proliferation might be seen in several of the settings mentioned early in this essay. The brief observations that follow attempt to cast at least a narrow beam of light on the relationship of proliferation to strategic, distributional, and international institutional considerations.

The Central Strategic Balance[1]

Paradoxically, both central strategic inadequacy and central strategic immoderation can stimulate proliferation. Simply put, to the degree that the central balance is evolving in a way that diminishes the ability of the superpowers to provide convincingly for the security of previously sheltered smaller states, those states—especially one-time clients of the

[1]The 1980s Project will in the months ahead produce a major volume on alternative arrangements for managing strategic weapons and strategic relationships. The main concern of the several studies in the volume will be the central balance, but the ways in which that balance will affect and be affected by the threat or fact of nuclear proliferation will also be examined.

12

United States—may resort to independent means of assured security. Yet should the superpowers seek to preserve or improve their ability to provide security for others through their nuclear postures, a general climate conducive to proliferation will persist: perceptions of the salience and value of nuclear weapons will not dissipate, and the antiproliferation exhortations of the nuclear states will continue to ring hollow. Thus if nonproliferation were to be a major criterion in the future management of the central balance, two objectives would have to be reconciled: enhancement of the security of non-nuclear states and progress in constraining the nuclear appetites and prerogatives of the superpowers.

One cannot escape the fact that these two objectives are to some extent incompatible, implying that trade-offs would have to be made on the basis of judgments as to which objective deserves greater attention. For instance, a unilateral or negotiated reduction in tactical nuclear weapons and other ''forward-based systems'' would improve the general climate of the nonproliferation norm. But such a measure would also cause a number of states (e.g., South Korea, West Germany, Japan, Turkey, Taiwan) to ask themselves if it would not be imprudent to close the option of producing nuclear weapons.

While such trade-offs will have to be made—by either action or inaction—there are some developments that might promote both objectives or at least promote one without seriously undercutting the other. A comprehensive test ban would seem to fit this requirement. A pledge by the superpowers not to use nuclear weapons against the territories of states that neither possess their own nuclear weapons nor harbor those of other states might be another such measure. This action would symbolize a willingness on the part of the superpowers to accept constraints and would weaken, though certainly not dispel, the notion that nuclear weapons endow the possessor with decisive power over nonpossessors. Since the acquisition of nuclear weapons would constitute disqualification from the shelter of the pledge, opponents of proliferation within national debates could argue more effectively that security is jeopardized rather than enhanced by acquisition.[2]

[2]This measure could of course be made stronger still if all nuclear states could be induced to accede (India because of Pakistan; China because of Taiwan, Japan, and South Korea; Israel because of the Arabs) and if states that refuse to sign and ratify the Non-Proliferation Treaty are excluded from the list of formally proscribed nuclear targets.

Another way in which the management of the central strategic relationship might contribute to nonproliferation goals is through mutual quantitative reductions in American and Soviet central weapons systems. With attention increasingly focusing on the qualitative aspects of the strategic balance—and with reductions being regarded by many analysts as possibly destabilizing in this age of improving counterforce capabilities—sizable reductions are not likely to be given a top priority within the negotiations aimed at preserving the stability of the strategic balance. But strategists and arms controllers tend to overlook the psychological implications of their craft. Reductions, even at some cost in terms of stability, would instill in citizens the feeling that their world was improving, even if some strategic theorists could "prove" that it was not. Such a sentiment would hardly be decisive in dissuading determined proliferants. But it would bolster the nonproliferation norm in a general sense; it would partially deprive weapons proponents of their rationalization that the vertical growth of nuclear capabilities at the center justified acquisition by others; and it would signify that the superpowers did not insist that only others bear the costs of an effective international antiproliferation strategy. Properly conceived and implemented, reductions—such as in land-based missiles, which are becoming increasingly vulnerable anyway—need not contribute to the anxieties of societies that derive nuclear security from either of the superpowers.

The future of the central balance and strategic arms control will not only influence but also be influenced by the prospects and dynamics of proliferation. The further spread of nuclear weapons could create new ambiguities and, conceivably, disequilibria in what has become a relatively stable strategic relationship. In particular, the expectation in both Moscow and, perhaps less acutely, Washington that more states will go nuclear might cause renewed interest in civil defense and missile defense systems to protect Soviet and American societies from the weapons of the new nuclear states, an unwelcome development from the standpoint of maintaining a stable central balance. Yet by eschewing strategic defense altogether, the United States and the Soviet Union would be increasing the rewards of proliferation, since any country willing and able to make the investment could realistically aspire to a minimum deterrence capability vis-à-vis the nuclear giants. The prospects for controlling developments in strategic antisubmarine warfare

(ASW) may well be limited by the fact that neither superpower will agree to deprive itself of the means of protection against the strategic submarines of future proliferants. In short, the superpowers will struggle to maintain their duopoly, but at the same time the partnership may become increasingly strained.

Proliferation and the Political Economy of North-South Relations[3]

To most strategists and statesmen in the industrialized ("Northern") world, the specter of proliferation evokes three deep concerns: (1) a general fear that the spread of nuclear weapons will make nuclear war—sometime, somewhere—more likely, (2) a set of more specific fears about the consequences of particular proliferation contingencies on one's own security, and (3) a set of fears—both specific and general— that proliferation will have a debilitating effect on the prudential management of East-West security relationships, particularly the Soviet-American nuclear equilibrium.

It so happens that a number of the states that appear on everyone's proliferation "worry list" are developing ("Southern") countries. They are the objects of concern, however, not because they are Southern but because they are potential proliferants. They are potential proliferants not because they are Southern but because of their desire for greater national stature and, in some cases, because of particular security needs. The less entangled a potential proliferant may be in Northern security affairs, the less prominent are fears 2 and 3, although fear 1 persists. If West Germany and Japan were seriously contemplating the acquisition of nuclear weapons, Pakistan, Brazil, and Indonesia would be footnotes. The proliferation worries of present nuclear weapons states conform to patterns of security concerns, not to patterns of relative levels of economic development.

There are those who would argue that proliferation is an issue on

[3]The relationship between the industrialized countries (the "North") and the underdeveloped countries (the "South") is a matter of central interest in the 1980s Project. Because this relationship pervades so many issue areas, nearly all of the work of the Project will take it into account. As well, a number of forthcoming volumes will deal directly with many aspects of the North-South relationship in the next decade and beyond.

which a bargain can be struck relating to the distribution of wealth between the developed and underdeveloped worlds. The only arguable way that the issue of proliferation could work to the material advantage of the developing world would be if the industrialized states were to conclude either that they could buy off potential proliferants more or less directly with resource transfers or that economic impoverishment breeds proliferation and should therefore be rectified. If the developed states were to reach the first conclusion, however, the most likely proliferants would logically be made the principal beneficiaries: South Africa, the Koreas, Taiwan, Iran, the Arabs, and Brazil—hardly the neediest of Southern states. No bargain. If the nuclear states were to reach the second conclusion, the economically deprived might be the immediate beneficiaries, but the serious nuclear candidates—being economically quite well off—would be last in the income redistribution line. Redistribution goals would be furthered, but proliferation would hardly be impeded. Again, no bargain.

But these are moot considerations, for neither of these conclusions is likely to be reached by policymakers in the industrialized countries. There is little evidence that nuclear weapons bring wealth (China, India, and Great Britain have nuclear weapons; West Germany, Japan, Sweden, and Canada do not), and there is little reason to believe that economic return is an important proliferation incentive. To the extent that economic conditions figure in the spread of nuclear weapons, economic success rather than failure is likely to contribute to proliferation. The Koreas, Iran, Saudi Arabia, Brazil, South Africa, and Nigeria are likely to define the rule; even India, though most of its huge population is impoverished, is in the process of becoming a major industrial power. When states are successful in increasing their power, prospects, and prosperity, the lack of nuclear weapons is a more conspicuous deficiency than it is in the context of weakness, stagnation, and poverty. Acquiring nuclear weapons is not an act of desperation; it is an act of "arriving" on the nuclear front as one has arrived or is arriving on the other fronts of national power and success. Why should the developed states believe that they can retard proliferation by helping those who might acquire nuclear weapons—in particular or in general—when the very states that appear most likely to acquire nuclear weapons have been the recipients of substantial assistance or have been doing quite well on their own?

These observations notwithstanding, the relationship between proliferation and the achievement of Southern goals may be profoundly important, though not in the way usually considered. The spread of nuclear weapons could seriously undercut the principal instrument of Southern strategy, solidarity, and could damage chances for the achievement of those particular Southern goals that are fostered by a tranquil, stable regional/local security environment. Future proliferants will in general be motivated primarily by a desire to enhance national power and prestige and by security interests. In the case of the typical Southern proliferant, these motivations will stem from a desire to achieve recognition as a global or regional power and from regional security interests. The important point is that the security objectives will be essentially regional in nature, not global: regional military preponderance (Iran, Brazil), a means of relieving regional conventional security concerns (South Africa, South Korea), or a means of relieving regional nuclear security concerns (Pakistan, Taiwan).

It stands to reason that the effects of proliferation in the developing world will also be primarily regional/local in nature. Indeed, the acquired nuclear weapons will ordinarily be targeted at fellow Southerners and only fellow Southerners, if for no other reason than simply that the radii of effective delivery system will be strictly regional/local. In the absence of nuclear weapons, intra-Southern antagonists have evinced an ability to keep security problems from precluding unified positions on North-South issues. This would be substantially more difficult to do should those security problems take on a nuclear character. Knowledge that one's own society and economy may be thoroughly devastated by one's neighbor can have a corrosive effect on one's capacity to identify and pursue common interests with that neighbor. Moreover, individual developing states might look to their former Northern "benefactors" for security in the face of increasingly dangerous Southern neighbors.

The achievement of nuclear status by some Southern states would reinforce or accelerate political hierarchical tendencies within the South. Political hierarchy does not in itself contradict solidarity on traditional North-South issues. But insofar as the acquisition of nuclear weapons will have rewards in terms of international respect, access, and privilege, the segregation of the South into nuclear haves and have-nots will have splintering effects far beyond the nuclear security area. To believe that any increase in the prestige of particular Southern proliferants would somehow elevate their non-nuclear brethren in the South is to

17

swallow the most indigestible of all self-serving national rationalizations for acquiring nuclear weapons.[4]

Other undesirable aspects of Southern proliferation are the diversion of resources to the development of nuclear arsenals and associated delivery systems and, of course, the possibility of nuclear conflict itself. It is hard to imagine how eventualities such as these would enhance solidarity or contribute to development goals. I do not mean to imply that particular Southern states cannot benefit from producing nuclear weapons. Those interested in greater national recognition, increased regional influence, and improved security positions may find that developing nuclear weapons can be helpful, at least in the short run. But such returns from going nuclear would come largely at the expense of neighbors whose security and freedom from regional bullying were diminished.

If nuclearization might be injurious to Southern goals, threatened nuclearization might evoke not Northern generosity but an antiproliferation strategy conceived by the nuclear states, with the interests of the developing states a secondary consideration at best. It is in the long-range interest of the developing world to resist the spread of nuclear weapons and to seize the initiative (through such measures as regional denuclearization and regional fuel-cycle construction) in making operational a nonproliferation strategy appropriate for the South.

Proliferation as an Institutional Challenge[5]

Being neither strictly an arms control issue nor strictly an energy issue, nuclear proliferation confronts us with an unusually complex set of institutional needs. To begin with, a number of technical services to support worldwide the maintenance of a safe civilian (i.e., "peaceful") nuclear power industry ought to remain or become institutionalized: safeguarding nuclear material from diversion; and assisting in safety, physical security, and managerial performance in accounting for materials. Strengthening these as internationalized services would serve to

[4]On the other hand, who would have thought that a 500 percent increase in the price of oil would make heroes out of the OPEC nations throughout much of the developing world?

[5]At a later stage in the course of the 1980s Project, an intensive effort will be made to develop a set of ideas concerning desirable international institutional arrangements in general.

establish—and in time raise—minimal standards for the nuclear power industry worldwide and to bolster international confidence in the objective maintenance of those standards.

More controversial is the question of the regulation of the international market in nuclear technology—deciding what may be sold by whom, to whom, and under what terms. A market regulated by the exporters alone would weaken the perceived legitimacy of nonproliferation as an international norm and would be no less fragile than most cartels. But institutionalizing control with nuclear importers also participating would leave the regulatory function vulnerable to the nuclear power appetites of the more numerous importers. While there is no easy way out of this dilemma, perhaps the most sensible arrangement would be one in which market regulation was institutionalized globally, but where the exporters would set and maintain their own common standards as insurance against insufficient international regulation. In any case, the obvious fit between the need for international technical services mentioned above (which clearly ought to be institutionalized on as wide a basis as possible) and the need for market regulation suggests that the latter should join the former under one global institutional umbrella.

Can an institution properly perform these technical and market-regulating functions while also *promoting* the expansion of nuclear power—long the first duty of the International Atomic Energy Agency (IAEA)?[6] It might be argued that unless the institution can reward participation with access to nuclear technology, there will be few incentives to join. But the institution could refrain from promoting nuclear power and still offer advantages to members if the nuclear exporters agree to refuse to enter into transactions with nonmembers. In turn, to induce all exporters to participate, members who are importers might be obligated to buy only from other members. Realistically, for access to the nuclear market to be the principal inducement for participation, the United States and most of the other key exporters would have to make the commitment not to deal with any country that did not accept the operating standards, safeguards, and market regulations embodied in the institution.

Assuming that one of the main purposes of international energy

---

[6] ". . . to accelerate and enlarge the contribution of atomic energy to peace, health and prosperity throughout the world. . . ." (Article II of the IAEA Statute)

institutions in the next decade will be to foster development of alternatives to petroleum, a nonproliferation institution should perhaps be divorced from energy institutions. If it is not, there would be considerable danger that the institution designed to safeguard and regulate the growth of nuclear power would find itself also with the mission of promoting nuclear power. While it was once thought that the best way to forestall the spread of nuclear weapons was to foster the spread of peaceful nuclear technology, experience has shown the flaws in this concept. A nonproliferation institution should neither promote nuclear power nor be part of some future international energy institution.

Some connection with the network of international arms control institutions, however, might be desirable. The technical resources and the intrusive principles and practices of a nonproliferation institution could be adapted to other possible arms control processes of the future—e.g., on-site verification of warhead- and range-test limitations, launcher limitations, or reduction accords. (The resistance of the IAEA to expanding its arms control functions has been due primarily to the concern that the central mission of promoting nuclear power would thereby be weakened.) The principal drawback to creating formal links with a network of international arms control institutions would be the risk that the nonproliferation agenda would become a hostage to progress on other arms control fronts (e.g., SALT), and vice versa. Then again, the expanded use of a nonproliferation institution as an international verification resource—applied primarily to the weapons programs of the nuclear states—might mitigate its discriminatory character.

Should an institution designed to impede proliferation be independent from the central political bodies of the international system? Put differently, should institutional arrangements emphasize or deemphasize the politics of nonproliferation? If the achievement of nonproliferation goals requires both institutional legitimacy and the capacity to broker inducements and sanctions linked to other areas of international activity—aid, energy cooperation, membership in various functional institutions—there may well be a need to involve the UN. Linkages and legitimacy are inherently political phenomena; an independent and essentially technocratic institution may be incompetent to develop either. Moreover, if, as suggested above, some future nonproliferation institution increasingly assumes additional international technical arms control services, some connection with global politico-security organs—in particular the Security Council and the Conference of the

Committee on Disarmament—would be needed. Finally, there would have to be some means of recourse in the event of irregularities or violations of the regulatory and safeguard provisions of a nonproliferation institution. The alternative to specifying constituted international authority (namely, the Security Council) as the means of recourse would be to hope that the superpowers or the nuclear exporters would consult and act in the event of noncompliance. Not only would the latter probably not happen, but dependence upon such a vague and hegemonic arrangement would offend the very non-nuclear states whose participation is sought. As distrusted as the Security Council might be, its charter is relatively clear and its potential for abusing the interests of small and non-nuclear states is circumscribed.

Still, there is much to be said for making a nonproliferation institution independent from global political bodies. Doing so would lessen the risk that proliferation functions might become hostage to the agenda of political institutions that proved incapable of conducting international business. In fact, institutional independence might permit greater opportunity to disguise as technical matters nonproliferation issues of a political—or potentially politicized—nature. Perhaps the best formula would be for the UN to provide the mandate for a nonproliferation institution, to authorize collaboration with other institutions to induce participation and compliance, and to provide political recourse in the event of violation of safeguard or market regulatory provisions, but to have no role in the policies and operations of the nonproliferation institution.

Nonproliferation—as a set of norms, rules, and practices—might lend itself to institutionalization at a regional level. The strengthening of regional security apparatus in general might help reduce both the incentives and the impact of proliferation within a region, based on the nuclear-free-zone concept or regional ''no-use'' pledges. Regional efforts could reinforce global institutions by eschewing nuclear commerce that is not conducted according to international regulations. And because multilateral participation in the ownership and operation of nuclear facilities would substantially reduce the risk that individual countries would divert material from those facilities for use in making weapons, regional fuel centers could be safeguarded to the satisfaction of the wider international community through international verification rather than some form of international presence. Global and regional nonproliferation institutions should be seen not as alternatives but as

21

mutually beneficial arrangements aimed both at strengthening norms against the acquisition of weapons and at making departure from those norms technically more difficult.

* * * * * * * * * * *

The studies that follow explore aspects of the issue of proliferation at much greater depth than have these few pages. They comprise the substance of this volume—this essay being only an attempt to highlight the respects in which those studies relate to each other and to questions that their authors were not asked to consider, but which are the topics of yet other 1980s Project studies.

Discouraging Proliferation in the Next Decade and Beyond

Ted Greenwood

ONE

Nuclear Weapons and National Purposes

Governments view nuclear weapons, like other components of military force, as instruments and symbols of power that can be manipulated to promote their interests. These interests may include protecting national sovereignty or the power of a ruling regime, enhancing diplomatic influence, protecting or extending economic interests, supporting allies, thwarting foes and potential foes, and generally bolstering national power and position within the hierarchy of nations. Nuclear weapons might, in some cases, also be thought to improve a government's ability to influence a particular situation by signaling its interest in an issue or geographical region, indicating its intention to participate actively in the resolution of a conflict or dispute, or projecting a national image that contributes to structuring the psychological environment of international diplomacy in a way that will maximize its interests. Those within a government who contemplate the acquisition of a nuclear capability will consider the extent to which it would contribute to or detract from these objectives and will weigh that against domestic political considerations and such countervailing factors as economic cost. Judgment about the utility of nuclear weapons for more narrowly military purposes would also be an important component of the choice, but would not likely dominate.

If national governments or the international community are to act effectively to impede the process of nuclear proliferation, these motivations for states to acquire nuclear weapons must be investigated and understood. What issues are likely to be dominant in a state's consideration of its nuclear option? Under what circumstances will states see their primary interests promoted by a nuclear capability? And when will the opposite be the case? What are the means available to influence these perceptions? These are the primary questions that must be addressed in the formulation of a strategy to inhibit nuclear proliferation, and they form the basis for this analysis.

The possession of nuclear weapons by a state implies the threat and possibility of employing them in combat, but governments would prefer not to use them that way. Political objectives achieved by threat or coercion are preferable to the same outcome achieved by war. This is probably even truer in the nuclear context than with respect to the employment of conventional forces. A strong aversion to the use[1] of nuclear weapons has developed since 1945, when responsible American officials had few qualms about using nuclear weapons to destroy two Japanese cities. This aversion is shared not only by all current nuclear powers but also by non-nuclear states around the world. Some societies and their governments, whether for ethical, religious, humanitarian, or other reasons, simply do not regard rapid, concentrated, and extensive destruction as an acceptable instrument of policy. Others fear nuclear retaliation. All share a strong unwillingness to traverse a firmly entrenched behavioral barrier and thereby unleash powerful emotional and psychological forces that would lead to uncertain but potentially very dangerous results.

This aversion does not guarantee that nuclear weapons will never be used. Indeed, they might be. But that would constitute a failure of policy. Nuclear use, if it occurred, would probably result from an accident, a miscalculation, an unauthorized act of a military commander, or the military and emotional escalation of a crisis situation to the point where rational judgment was overwhelmed by panic or vindictive passion. As an outcome of systematic, rational planning, nuclear use seems very unlikely.

The reluctance to *use* nuclear weapons is, however, not directly

---

[1]The concept of nuclear *use* is a troublesome one. Nuclear weapons are, of course, used as threats, as instruments of power, and as protectors of various national interests without actually being detonated with destructive or coercive intent. If the term is employed with the former meanings, however, no convenient word is available to convey the latter meaning. For the purposes of this essay, the term *use of nuclear weapons* will always have the more limited meaning of detonation with destructive or coercive intent. The terms *political use* or *coercive use* will be employed to suggest uses that do not include detonation.

26

translatable into a reluctance on the part of non-nuclear states to *acquire* them. The most salient consideration in the choice of whether to obtain a nuclear capability will be its political, not its military, utility: that is, the extent to which the implied or explicit threats that are or can be associated with nuclear possession will be, on balance, beneficial in influencing the attitudes and actions of other states. But the reluctance to use nuclear weapons is not irrelevant to proliferation. Under most circumstances, national leaders are likely to favor the acquisition of nuclear weapons only if they do not think they will be drawn into actually using these weapons. A small number of beleaguered states might be most likely to acquire nuclear weapons or to acknowledge an existing capability precisely when they are most likely to use them to prevent their own destruction. But even they would be less willing to prepare for that contingency or at least to prepare for it openly if they thought that the likelihood of eventual use would thereby increase. To the extent that nuclear possession is perceived as likely to result in nuclear use, nuclear weapons are less attractive.

THE NATURE OF THE PROLIFERATED WORLD

But what of the likelihood of nuclear war in a world in which many more countries possess nuclear capability? Leaders of future nuclear states, disputing factions within such states, and even revolutionaries or terrorists might well share the aversion to nuclear use or at least calculate that their interest lies in acting as if they did. Command and control, communications, and physical security might be good enough to preclude accidents, miscalculations, unauthorized use, or theft. A proliferated world might be no more unstable against escalation to nuclear war than the current one; in fact, the risk of escalation to nuclear levels might serve to reduce the prevalence of conventional war. As the United States and the Soviet Union have found, the specter of nuclear conflagration usually encourages caution. In short, therefore, a proliferated world might be no more dangerous than our own.

But there is another possibility. Peoples, nations, and political leaders have sufficiently diverse cultural heritages and ideologies that there is no assurance that future leaders of nuclear states will not regard nuclear weapons as simply equivalent to other military instruments. Particularly as the memory of the horror of Hiroshima and Nagasaki fades, the

27

aversion to nuclear use may decline. With nuclear weapons available to large numbers of states, the opportunities for escalation of conventional conflict to nuclear war and for nonbelligerents in a conflict to use their own nuclear weapons to spark a so-called catalytic war may increase. At least the statistical probability of nuclear accident, miscalculation, or unauthorized use rises as the number of nuclear states increases. In the course of a violent national upheaval within an unstable nuclear state, military factions or revolutionary organizations might seize and subsequently use nuclear weapons. In a proliferated world, nuclear warfare might become thinkable, even commonplace, and perhaps also anonymous.

Individual judgments about the likely result of proliferation will differ, since no proposed theory of the future can be proven. While such judgments inevitably color views about the seriousness of proliferation and about what should be done to impede it, they do not provide a sufficient basis for determining policy. Equally important is the range of uncertainty around the best estimate. Even those who, like myself, conclude that the likely result of greater proliferation would be a world not much or perhaps any more prone to nuclear war than today's world must admit that the uncertainties are large and mostly involve the possibility of greater danger. The chances that proliferation will reduce the likelihood of nuclear war are quite small. The risks therefore, are large—large enough to preclude much serious advocacy of widespread proliferation, large enough to make worthwhile efforts to understand the underlying dynamics of nuclear proliferation and to seek means to inhibit it, and, most important, large enough to justify attention and preventive action by individual states and the international community.

Two possible patterns of proliferation appear to involve the greatest risks for nuclear use or war. The first is proliferation to particular categories of states. Those advanced industrial states, such as West Germany and Japan, that were the major sources of concern a decade or so ago are in fact probably the countries that involve the least risk. The greatest risks involve those states, such as Israel, South Africa, South Korea, and Taiwan, that confront major challenges to their borders, to the legitimacy of their regimes, or to their very existence as sovereign entities. In a seemingly hopeless situation their nuclear weapons might actually be used in an act of desperation. Another category of high-risk states includes those prone to terrorist activity or revolutionary change.

In these cases nuclear use by the government itself is of less concern than seizure and subsequent use by a variety of non-state entities. A final category includes states prone to autocratic rule by charismatic leaders who might not share the usual aversion to nuclear use or be sufficiently restrained by such institutional mechanisms as exist elsewhere.

The second dangerous possibility is proliferation at a rapid rate. The world could probably adjust to a moderate rate. But rapid proliferation could cause instabilities that might be too great for political systems and institutions to handle, making nuclear use or nuclear war more likely. Thus any strategy for nonproliferation should especially attempt to prevent a rapid spread of nuclear weapons and to avert acquisition by states in the high-risk categories.

Nuclear proliferation will also have important effects on world and regional stability for reasons not directly related to nuclear use. The mere possession of nuclear weapons by certain states could radically alter international perceptions and threaten global arrangements. If nuclear weapons were acquired by states such as Japan or West Germany, whose military capabilities and political allegiances were particularly salient to local security arrangements, by states that are unable or unwilling to build a secure deterrent force, or by states whose self-image and international role would thereby be radically and perhaps unpredictably altered, the result might well be greater uncertainty in political relationships, the unraveling of existing security arrangements, and decreased international political stability.

These changes, uncertainties, and instabilities would not necessarily lead to a nuclear way. They might or might not be considered undesirable. Today's major military and economic powers would almost certainly deem them detrimental. Those who benefit from the status quo naturally prefer stability and certainty to instability and uncertainty. Those who might expect to benefit from change, however, might think the potential gains outweigh the potential risks. New nuclear states, after all, might expect to find themselves more shielded from external challenge and therefore more secure. They might also acquire greater political power, which could be expected eventually to alter the distribution of global wealth in their favor.

These introductory comments notwithstanding, this study is not primarily an investigation of the *results* of nuclear proliferation. These will be considered only where they illuminate other subjects of more immediate concern.[2] The main concern here will be to analyze the various incentives and disincentives—involving both security and political considerations—that will affect states' decisions about whether or not to acquire nuclear weapons.

THE NATURE OF PROLIFERATION

In the 32 years since the first nuclear test was made by the United States, 5 additional states have detonated nuclear devices; of these 6, all but India have developed and deployed rather impressive and costly, although quite different, nuclear weapons delivery capabilities. While there is no way to know how many more states have been prevented from acquiring nuclear weapons by their lack of technological or financial resources, there is no doubt that many states with all the necessary capabilities have chosen to refrain. Nuclear weapons have spread far more slowly than other military and most civilian technologies, including nuclear electricity generation. This record suggests that at least for most nations that have had available the means to develop or acquire nuclear weapons, either the incentives to do so have not been very strong or the disincentives have been stronger. Identifying the incentives and disincentives for the existing nuclear states and investigating whether a different pattern can be expected among potential proliferators will be the first task of this study.

The discussion will then turn to the means by which individual states and the international community can influence nuclear incentives and disincentives. The particularly important subject of the management of the international nuclear industry is addressed separately, followed by an analysis of nuclear acquisition, use, and threat by non-state entities. Finally, a general strategy for decreasing incentives and increasing disincentives is proposed and applied to four special categories of states. The strategy relies on the following policy instruments:

- Maintaining or strengthening existing security guarantees and extending them when appropriate

[2]In a forthcoming 1980s Project volume, David Gompert will explore the question of what a world with widespread proliferation might be like and how it ought to be managed.

- Working to resolve or stabilize regional disputes that might stimulate proliferation
- Strengthening the international behavioral norm against the acquisition of nuclear weapons
- Acting through international markets to dissuade states from acquiring their own sensitive nuclear facilities
- Replacing technical and economic barriers against access to nuclear materials with institutional and political barriers against using those materials to make weapons
- Reducing the prestige and symbolic importance of nuclear weapons in world politics
- In special cases, satisfying some of the ambitions of near-nuclear or potential nuclear states or non-state entities
- Applying moral suasion to potential proliferators
- Physicially protecting weapons and weapons material
- Actively suppressing nuclear-prone, non-state entities.

First, though, the term *nuclear proliferation* must be defined. For purposes of this discussion, a state will be considered to have acquired nuclear weapons only if it has unambiguously convinced the world that it has done so. To date, a nuclear detonation has been the standard signal. In the future, however, an official declaration of possession by some states might be equally convincing. An avowed peaceful nuclear detonation such as India's would still demonstrate a weapons capability, since so-called peaceful nuclear explosives (PNEs) are technically indistinguishable from explosives that can be used for or developed into military weapons. A nuclear detonation is a dramatic, unequivocal, and irrevocable threshold act. It will serve as the functional definition of nuclear proliferation for the purposes of this paper.

It is, however, far from the whole story. A state can gain political benefits (or incur political costs) from a potential nuclear weapons capability as well as from a demonstrated capability. Any state with a large industrial infrastructure and many highly trained scientific and technical personnel has an obvious nuclear potential and in a few years could acquire weapons-grade materials for fabricating and testing an explosive. In the past, concern has largely been focused on such states.

31

More recently, however, attention has been directed toward states with medium or very modest scientific and industrial infrastructures. Even they can gain credibility as potential nuclear states, though not without considerable cost.

Such states could gradually acquire a civilian nuclear industry oriented toward electric power generation. In this way personnel would receive training in nuclear technologies and in handling nuclear materials. If spent reactor fuel was not exported, the result would be a gradually growing national inventory of plutonium that could, if removed from the spent fuel, be used to manufacture explosives. If the industry included an indigenous fuel reprocessing plant, or if fuel were reprocessed elsewhere and the fissile material returned, an inventory of readily available plutonium would be accumulated. If a uranium enrichment plant were acquired, another potential means of acquiring weapons-grade material would be available. The existence of trained personnel and of an accessible plutonium stockpile or uranium enrichment facilities would significantly reduce the lead time necessary to build a nuclear explosive once the decision was made to do so. This universally recognized fact infuses political significance into a state's decision to develop a nuclear power program. The anticipation of future weapons capability will have a significant effect on present attitudes of others.

A state with a strong scientific-industrial base or a growing nuclear industry can pursue an interesting strategy. It can hint subtly or openly that it already has nuclear weapons or a weapons development program, or it can suggest that it wants or intends to develop nuclear weapons. If it were inconceivable that the state could acquire materials and assemble the technical expertise needed to fabricate explosives, hints of this sort would have little or no political value. But once hints became credible, they could provide many of the potential advantages of a real capability with few of the liabilities. To the extent that other governments might wish to discourage the carrying out of the threat implied by credible hints, the hints themselves could become instruments of coercion or deterrence. Israel has been using such hints that way for years. If, as seems likely, increasing numbers of states come to pursue a similar strategy, a new and unsettling variety of uncertainty will be introduced into the international system.

A state that really wants an actual nuclear weapons capability could rely on a nuclear power industry as a source of weapons-grade fissile materials. It is not likely to do so, however, at least until reactors now under development which use weapons-grade materials for fuel or produce better-grade plutonium come into widespread use. The uranium use for fuel in current power reactors is insufficiently enriched in fissile isotopes to be used for weapons. Plutonium produced in the normal operation of these reactors could be used for explosives but has a lower content of fissile material than a weapons designer would ideally like. Its use would require more care and would result in lower yield and efficiency. Current power reactors could produce better-quality plutonium, but only by greatly reducing the amount of electricity generated. Another cost of such a policy might be a bureaucratic conflict between the weapons designers and the electric power utility operators, who would be loath to accept the required inefficiencies. Perhaps more important, diversion from a nuclear power industry would, for most states, have political drawbacks: the risks of detection by safeguards mechanisms or the cost of abrogating or ignoring safeguards agreements.

There is a much cheaper and easier route for most states, with or without a nuclear power industry, to obtain high-quality plutonium within 5 to 15 years. The time required would depend on the technical and industrial base of the country when the program was initiated. There are two requirements: one or more modest-sized, rather simply designed, heavy-water or graphite-moderated nuclear reactors using natural uranium fuel in a straightforward fuel assembly; and a small fuel reprocessing plant designed to extract plutonium at a rather high level of chemical purity from low-burnup, low-radioactive fuel. These requirements are far more modest than a commercial power reactor and a reprocessing plant designed to extract extremely high purity plutonium and uranium from very radioactive power reactor fuel. The existence of this opportunity is extremely important and not well appreciated by the general public, by many students of the proliferation problem, and even by planners in many potential nuclear states. The common assumption that barring theft or purchase, weapons-grade materials can only be or would most likely be acquired through a civilian nuclear power program is simply wrong. Relying on a plutonium production reactor and an unsophisticated reprocessing facility dedicated to a weapons program would be much quicker, easier, and cheaper.

The evolution of uranium enrichment technology could make available another straightforward route, this time to a uranium weapon.

But given the current state of technology, this would probably not be the chosen method for at least the next 5 to 10 years.

Even if weapons-grade material were available to a potential proliferant, an explosive device would still have to be produced. The difficulty of this task would depend on the quality and quantity of the plutonium available and the yield and efficiency of the weapon desired. Assuming that sufficient quantities of high-quality plutonium were available from the sort of dedicated facilities described, fabrication of an inefficient, low-yield explosive would be well within the resources of most states. A first nuclear detonation is not necessarily equivalent to or a demonstration of an actual weapons capability, however. Designing and building an efficient and deliverable weapon is considerably more difficult than creating a nuclear explosion. Whether a state would be satisfied with a crude explosive or instead feel that nothing short of an efficient and easily transportable weapon was worthwhile would depend on the objectives that the program was intended to serve. The number of nuclear tests required to provide confidence in the design of a true military weapon or to develop a number of different weapons tailored to particular functions would depend on the technical sophistication of the weapons designers. Independent of the technical requirements, the rate of testing also could be used as a political signal of intent and commitment to the development of a nuclear arsenal.

Nuclear weapons themselves have little military value and somewhat limited political value unless they can be delivered to a designated target. Any country can deliver a nuclear explosive by putting it in a railroad car or on a ship and moving it to an appropriate location. While this method may serve for some purposes as a perfectly satisfactory means of delivery and does provide any state possessing nuclear explosives with some credibility as an actual nuclear power, its political utility is much less than that of tailored military delivery systems. These can be distinguished by their ability to penetrate defenses, to strike at various ranges, to survive conventional or nuclear attacks, and to respond under various circumstances and against different target sets.

The incentives and disincentives for developing these various levels of capability will not be evaluated here in detail. States with only limited political objectives might be quite satisfied with a few nuclear tests and little or no investment in actual weapons or delivery systems. The cost of their nuclear programs would be quite modest. Other states, however, will want an actual weapons capability, perhaps because they think the benefits they seek from a nuclear program require the creation of a credible military force. For them the cost might be very high and would depend on the size of the force required; the range and design of delivery systems chosen; and the attention paid to command, control, and security.

The context within which any government thinks about exercising a nuclear option will be unique. The complex evaluative and decision-making process through which the many incentives and disincentives to acquire nuclear weapons are considered, judged, integrated, and argued about will be different in both structure and procedure for every state. In fact, the differences among national processes and institutions might well affect the decisions reached by particular governments. The only characteristic shared by all governments is the struggle of a central decision-making authority to control a large number of compartmentalized bureaucratic entities with disparate outlooks and, often, conflicting interests. Although for simplicity's sake the following discussion will frequently treat a state as a single utility-maximizing entity with attributes that actually reside only in people, the reader should not forget that this approach only approximates reality. It is, however, a useful approximation, since this study is primarily interested in the ultimate compromise or consensus achieved through intragovernmental deliberations—a combined view that may, for all practical purposes, be considered the view of the government or of the state.

Uniqueness is important in other respects as well. Every state's local and regional security concerns, its alliances or tensions with other states, its leaders' proclivity for caution or for risk taking, and its ambitions for enhanced political, economic, or military power will influence its decisions. While adopting the perspective of individual governments or their component parts, this discussion will not provide the detailed, country-specific analyses that would be required to reach informed judgments about the likelihood of particular states' acquiring nuclear weapons.[3] Analysis at the level of generality employed here does not lead to conclusions or predictions about which or even how many states will be nuclear in a given period of years or how that number can be changed by

---

[3]For such an analysis see George H. Quester, *The Politics of Nuclear Proliferation,* The Johns Hopkins Press, Baltimore, Md., 1973.

the exercise of recommended policy instruments. Ultimately, separate policy choices must be made with respect to each potential nuclear state. Fortunately the number of candidates is not yet so high as to overwhelm the analytical and decision-making capacity of governments. The present analysis should be useful in thinking about those choices and should provide insight into what to look for in detailed, state-specific analyses.

TWO

Security Objectives

Every government must strive to protect its territory from invasion or annexation, its sovereign independence from military or political challenge, and its interests from external threat. Some governments must also guard themselves against organized groups of their own subjects who seek their overthrow. Such efforts undertaken by a state to preserve and protect the status quo will be called *security objectives* for the purposes of this study. A state's own efforts to change the status quo—whether to increase its human, natural, or financial resources or to extend its power and influence—and whether or not it uses military force to do so, will be discussed below as *political objectives*.

Few governments either perceive no significant external challenge to their security interests or are content to rely for their protection on diplomacy or external security guarantees unsupported by their own military forces. Most governments have found a military establishment useful in supporting their political and diplomatic efforts and, when necessary, in fighting to defend sovereignty, territory, prerogative, or interest. Of the six current nuclear powers, only India has not readily admitted that it saw nuclear weapons as valuable additions to conventional military forces for pursuing security objectives and that this perception was an important motivation for developing a nuclear capability.

The extent to which security interests encourage or discourage the acquisition of nuclear weapons can best be examined by distinguishing between (1) essentially regional security interests and (2) security interests that derive from the possibility of confrontation with major military powers with global interests. Regional security interests include protection against challenges by neighboring or regional states that seek to revise territorial boundaries, that impede traditional passage over land or through ocean straits, or that seek to overthrow a government or interfere with its activities. Saudi Arabia's security problems with respect to Iraq or Israel, South Africa's anxiety about a challenge from black Africa, Taiwan's concerns with China, or Colombia's military competition with Venezuela are all examples of regional security issues.

Global security interests include the possibility of challenges, either direct or through interference in regional or domestic affairs, by global military powers. Examples are Saudi Arabia's or African states' apprehensions about the Soviet Union, the United States, and perhaps Western European states; Eastern Europe's concerns with the Soviet Union; and Caribbean or South American countries' anxiety about American intervention. The Soviet Union's threat to Japan appears to pose a regional security problem because of the two countries' geographic proximity, but the problem is more accurately considered global because both countries have worldwide interests at stake.

Another important security interest, that of general international stability, really fits into neither category. Many states do not feel imminent or serious security threats and, whether or not they are part of an alliance system, consider the overall climate and stability of their geographical region or the international system as their primary security interest. Canada, Sweden, Switzerland, and many countries in Latin America and the Pacific fall into this category. Security considerations offer them no incentives to acquire nuclear weapons; in fact, to the extent that their going nuclear would encourage others to do so, they feel a strong disincentive. They see a strategy of nonproliferation as a way to prevent the deterioration of global and regional arrangements conducive to their own security. Their attitudes are not based so much upon moral rectitude as upon perceptions of long-term self-interest.

REGIONAL SECURITY INTERESTS

Many non-nuclear states face problems of national security within their regions which seem likely to provide the major incentives for developing nuclear weapons. Whether in the Middle East, South America, Southeast Asia, Africa, or the Asian subcontinent, the major threat to

most governments, other than from domestic dissidents and revolutionaries, is from nearby states. For many states, these regional
threats provide the overriding, although not the only, motivation to build
and strengthen conventional forces. They do not, however, always
translate into incentives to obtain nuclear weapons; in fact, they sometimes translate into disincentives. The present task is to identify why
regional security considerations make some states see nuclear weapons
as an asset and others see them as a liability.

In a bilateral or regional conflict in which no state possesses nuclear
weapons, the more vulnerable state(s) would appear to have the greater
incentive to obtain a nuclear capability or to hint at that possibility. Their
enormous destructive power makes nuclear weapons appear to many to
be military equalizers. If not equalizers, they could at least be expected
to assist a challenged state in protecting the status quo. A state with a
reasonably high level technical-industrial base and modest delivery
capability could relatively quickly and inexpensively acquire nuclear
weapons as a way to increase very significantly its available military
power. Even were other states to respond by going nuclear themselves, the weaker state might still be, or perceive itself to be, less
unequal and more secure than under the previous conventional imbalance.

However, since nuclear weapons are not likely to be considered
usable military forces, this might not always be true. Nations that see
themselves as weak and threatened must judge whether the acquisition
of nuclear weapons or hints of such acquisition are more likely to deter
potential opponents—and if so, what level of forces, deployed how,
would deter what sort of threatening military or political actions—than
to stimulate, for example, the initiation of preventive war. An em-
bryonic nuclear force is likely to be small, vulnerable, and a tempting
target for preemptive attack by nuclear or, more likely, conventional
forces. Command and control systems must be developed, and national
leaders must gain experience in dealing with them. Indeed, the prospect
of great instability and risk of conflict during the period of transition
from non-nuclear to nuclear status might dissuade weaker states from
acquiring nuclear weapons. Moreover, the weaker states would have to
assume that their adversaries would also acquire nuclear weapons. The
previous unequal balance might then be restored or be made more
unequal, but at an even higher level of potential violence.

Sometimes, as in the Middle East and southern Africa, weaker states challenge a status quo protected by a regionally dominant power. Their superior military power does not shield regionally dominant states from the possibility of repeated wars or provocation. Wars can be quite limited in extent or can be fought by a surrogate revolutionary or guerrilla organization; indeed, even full-scale wars normally are fought for political objectives and rarely progress to total defeat. Thus dominant powers in such instances might decide that nuclear weapons, either hinted at or actually deployed with signals that they might be used, would deter provocation and war more effectively than conventional forces.

Or, a regionally dominant state might be concerned that its own nuclear program might encourage its adversaries to follow suit and that both the unstable transition period and the final equilibrium might be even more unfavorable than the previous situation. The state would fear losing the clear military superiority it enjoyed or was achieving before the introduction of nuclear weapons. Such concerns on the part of a regionally dominant or potentially dominant state not under direct challenge would weigh heavily against nuclear ambitions. The state also might lack the confidence that other governments that had been stimulated into a nuclear program would be willing or able to take the necessary precautions to prevent unauthorized use. These considerations would be particularly relevant to Iran, Brazil, and perhaps eventually to an emerging dominant power in black Africa.

The case of a long-standing confrontation or competition between non-nuclear states in which one discovers that the other is developing or has developed nuclear weapons may be no less uncertain, but for different reasons. If the non-nuclear state could possibly keep pace with or catch up with the state initiating the nuclear competition, the incentive to do so would probably be very strong. Acquisition by either Argentina or Brazil, Indonesia or Australia, or North or South Korea would likely spur the other to follow suit rapidly. Where the prospects are low for keeping pace with or catching up with the nuclear program of a regional rival, the incentive to try may be lower. In either case, the response of a state to the introduction of nuclear weapons into its region will depend importantly on its expectations of how its adversary will put its capability to use and on the availability of political and military alliances with global powers. How Pakistan, for example, will weigh these factors remains to be seen.

Even if there were no evidence of an actual weapons program, a government that believed its regional rival would inevitably acquire a nuclear capability might feel compelled to begin its own program. It might attempt to achieve a nuclear capability first, to start a more gradual program designed to keep pace with but not overly stimulate the rival's activities, or to develop a civilian nuclear program that would reduce the lead time following a future decision. Each of these programs could be secret or open, depending on the signals that the country wished to send to its rival, its allies, and perhaps its suppliers of nuclear equipment and technology. Because of the possibility of such an anticipatory response by one government to a rival's expected intentions, any state with a nuclear power program but no plans for either a weapons program or a policy of credible hints would be well advised to persuade others forthrightly of its own good intentions. Rivals might otherwise mutually and perhaps unwittingly reinforce each other's nuclear propensities because of ambiguity and misperceptions; Argentina and Brazil might well be doing this now. Indonesia and Australia could become involved in a similar vicious circle in the future.

Any state engaged in a border dispute or regional confrontation with a nuclear-armed state would have an incentive to develop its own nuclear capability. The purposes would be both to neutralize the political and military advantage of the opponent's nuclear weapons and to deter attack by conventional forces. While the credibility of a nuclear response to a conventional attack would vary from one instance to another, the uncertainty itself would be an important deterrent. A potential attacker could not be sure that a conventional incursion would not be met with nuclear resistance or retaliation. This incentive is probably quite strong in a case such as India vis-à-vis China or perhaps Iran vis-à-vis India, where both antagonists have nearly equal conventional military power and have similar, competitive political ambitions. In the absence of American security guarantees, this motivation might be decisive in causing Taiwan to develop nuclear capability.

There is a countervailing argument, however. A state in conflict with a nuclear power and unprotected by alliances with another nuclear power might feel, at least until it had deployed a secure second-strike capability, that a nuclear capability might only encourage a preemptive nuclear attack. An adversary might be less reluctant to launch a nuclear attack against a nuclear opponent it could disable than against a non-nuclear state. Nonetheless, since the threat of such an attack would probably not be very credible, this argument is not likely to be decisive. In cases where it would apply, its effect might be to encourage a clandestine nuclear program accompanied by hints rather than an overt program accompanied by threats.

The leaders of a state whose regional security is likely to deteriorate over the years might see the development of nuclear weapons as a way to counteract hostile forces and arrest or reverse the deterioration. Two particular sets of circumstances that might lead to this conclusion by a government are worth identifying. In one instance a state might face gradual but seemingly relentless political isolation within the international community as well as forces that seek to overthrow its government. South Africa, Rhodesia, and Taiwan fit this description. Except for its American support, Israel, too, could qualify. These states would probably not want to use nuclear weapons, but rather would see the uncertainty and changed psychological environment that resulted from their acquisition as sufficient to deter hostile acts by opponents. They might also expect nuclear possession to encourage external powers to intervene in a way that would protect the status quo. But acquiring nuclear weapons might lead to near-total isolation and greater pressure from adversaries who might either initiate their own nuclear programs or be less reluctant to employ nuclear threats. The great danger of these states' acquiring nuclear weapons derives from the possibility that if nuclear deterrence were to fail, the beleaguered government might find itself losing a conventional war without any hope of outside assistance. It might then use its nuclear arsenal out of desperation. These various disadvantages of nuclear weapons might encourage isolated and besieged states to eschew an overt nuclear program and adopt instead a strategy of credible hinting. Israel openly pursues that course; Taiwan and South Africa may follow suit.

The second set of circumstances in which governmental perception of long-term deterioration of a state's regional security position could be a powerful incentive to its going nuclear is that of the unraveling of existing alliances and security guarantees. Especially if a government had depended on a pledge of ultimate protection with nuclear weapons, any weakening in that guarantee, whether real or perceived, could prompt a decision to secure its own defense by producing nuclear weapons. But the same analysis would apply where security guarantees did not involve a nuclear umbrella. Whether because of official disillusionment or public sentiment, a weakening of American security guarantees to, for example, Pakistan, Iran, Australia, or South Korea could stimulate significant domestic pressure to acquire nuclear weapons. The withdrawal of foreign-based troops or tactical nuclear weapons from a state without its government's prior and willing consent could also cause this reaction, as it would in South Korea, for example. The incentives here seem so strong that they should figure prominently in any American assessment of alliance commitments and force deployments.

Nuclear weapons might sometimes be considered alternatives to conventional weapons. Particularly if a state cannot either afford to buy the conventional weapons it thinks it needs or find a willing supplier, it might turn to nuclear weapons. These could be deliverable by fairly unsophisticated means and could in fact be faster, easier, and cheaper for a state to build itself than the sort of advanced conventional hardware that would be required to provide any reasonable capability against a well-armed adversary. Since states do not normally expect to use nuclear weapons, however, potential proliferators would usually view them as additions rather than alternatives to conventional forces.

A domestic tradition of violent political change or of military intervention in national politics might also discourage a government from acquiring nuclear weapons. The government of a nation with such a tradition might be unsure of its ability to control nuclear weapons or prevent them from falling into the hands of political opponents or dissident military factions who could find them a significant source of power or even a usable instrument during an attempted coup d'état. It may also be uncertain of its ability to prevent the military from turning a first test or a modest test program into a significant military capability. In either case, the government might be somewhat reluctant to exercise the weapons option in the first place. Alternatively, national leaders in such countries might feel confident, perhaps incorrectly, that they could control their military and deployed nuclear weapons, but still might not trust the ability to do so of their possible successors. The extent to which this perception might be a restraining influence is highly uncertain. National leaders sometimes prefer to enhance their own power and prestige rather than protect the long-term interests of their country.

It is unlikely, as will be explained further below, that a small terrorist group or even a large revolutionary movement would seek to obtain nuclear weapons. Nonetheless, the possibility that such a non-state entity might steal nuclear weapons or material or threaten to use them against the state would doubtless damp the nuclear enthusiasm of governments unable to control revolutionary or terrorist groups within or near their borders. If a non-state group were known or suspected to have obtained nuclear weapons or significant amounts of weapons-grade material, a state might react with a nuclear weapons program of its own. Whether it would do so depends on the nature of the suspected non-state entity, other states' responses to the nuclear threat, and the implications of a nuclear response for relations with other states.

A nuclear response to a nuclear urban guerrilla group would be inappropriate and useless. Other responses, more closely resembling very strong police action, would be necessary. A nuclear response to a large, nationally oriented revolutionary movement operating out of a well-identified geographical area might be equally reasonable or un-reasonable as responding in kind to the nuclear program of a hostile neighbor. In the case of a non-state entity, however, other states, particularly those who had traditionally aided and abetted the group, might react to their client's nuclear activity by removing their support and thereby guaranteeing the group's elimination as a significant threat without the affected state's having to go nuclear. Particularly if the target state could achieve nuclear capability rapidly, supporters of the non-state group would have a major incentive to prevent it from acquiring nuclear weapons at all.

GLOBAL SECURITY INTERESTS

There are basically two sorts of global security interests: first, the desire to deter or protect against threats or military incursions by major powers with global interests, particularly the United States and the Soviet Union; second, the aim of increasing or decreasing the involvement of the superpowers in regional disputes and power balances.

Military intervention by nuclear states in non-nuclear states has been sufficiently common that many of the latter may be concerned about deterring such intervention in the future. Non-nuclear states would not be concerned primarily with deterring the use of nuclear weapons against them, although such use has been threatened on various oc-casions. The general aversion to nuclear use along with the usual ade-quacy of large-scale conventional power makes nuclear use against non-nuclear states barely credible today. The more important issue is the employment by formerly non-nuclear states of nuclear weapons for de-terrence of military intervention or of coercion with conventional forces.

Such nuclear deterrence might be effective only in circumstances in which the deterring state might plausibly be willing to use nuclear weapons for defense or retaliation. Nuclear defense would present few such circumstances because any government would be naturally reluctant to detonate nuclear weapons in or near its own territory. Even where geography and population density would make nuclear defense plausible, a government might still refrain because of the possibility that opponents may, in fact, be willing to put their expeditionary forces at risk or that these forces might themselves be nuclear-armed or assisted. The threat of nuclear retaliation in the face of conventional aggression would require a credible way to deliver warheads to a superpower's homeland. Even a commercial aircraft might suffice. Nonetheless, the prospect of a devastating nuclear counterretaliation by the superpower would probably deter the threatened state from escalating to nuclear conflict or even from seeing nuclear use as a potentially interesting option.

Although nuclear defense or retaliation against a superpower, and therefore nuclear deterrence of actions by a superpower, would not be particularly credible, the additional element of uncertainty introduced by nuclear possession should not be underestimated. Rarely are superpower interests challenged sufficiently by small states to warrant even a small risk of nuclear retaliation against either expeditionary forces or homeland. Therefore the possession of nuclear weapons by small- or medium-size states would probably serve as an effective deterrent against direct military intervention by a superpower, and states concerned about such intervention might find that option attractive.

Many states that are or feel threatened by a superpower are currently protected by an alliance with the other superpower. American allies in Western Europe and Japan and Soviet allies in Eastern Europe and Cuba are examples. The weakening of the superpower's guarantees to the governments of these states would affect their nuclear incentives no less than would the weakening of guarantees to states that are threatened by nonsuperpowers. Indeed, at least in Japan and West Germany, in the absence of American security guarantees, the domestic forces arguing for indigenous nuclear capability would probably be much stronger.

Whether the nuclearization of a regional dispute or power balance will tend to draw the superpowers in or to encourage them to steer clear is doubly ambiguous. In general, the introduction of nuclear weapons seems likely to reduce the chances that the United States or the Soviet

Union would seek unilateral advantage from local conflict and to increase the probability that they would intervene to defuse tensions. But circumstances can be imagined in which the opposite might be true. The emergence of a new nuclear power might encourage a superpower to participate actively in regional power balances in order either to gain the advantage of alliance with that state or to counter its increasing influence and power. Further, any set of expectations about the superpowers' reactions can have various consequences: it might act as a nuclear incentive, be a disincentive, or even have both effects. Israel, for example, might fear that the nuclearization of the Middle East would prompt the superpowers to impose a settlement inimical to its interest. It might also anticipate with approval action by the superpowers to prevent the outbreak of another war. Arab states, in contrast, might have precisely the opposite reaction.

RESERVATIONS AND CONCLUSIONS

Three factors ought to qualify the preceding arguments. First, complex strategic analysis of this sort may simply not be relevant to some decision makers who are unaccustomed to thinking in this way or who respond to more visceral instincts. Second, security incentives and disincentives may be perceived differently by different parts of a government. In some instances, the military or atomic energy bureaucracies might be able to move their country toward nuclear status, independent of their leaders' desires. Third, the relative significance of long- and short-term factors is unpredictable. The temporary political or military advantage of being the first and only nuclear power in a region might overshadow the more enduring problems of being only one of several nuclear powers. The planning horizon for most governments is at most 5 to 10 years, a time that may be shorter than would be required for regional adversaries to react by developing their own nuclear capability. Regionally dominant states in particular probably need less time and effort to develop nuclear weapons than do their less powerful neighbors and adversaries. To the extent that India's security problems vis-à-vis Pakistan motivated its nuclear program, for example, its perceptions of immediate advantages seem to have eclipsed the more abiding dangers inherent in Pakistan's own nuclear potential.

Notwithstanding these reservations, some tentative conclusions are possible. Those states that so far have been most capable of developing nuclear weapons appear in general to have the fewest security incentives for doing so. The United States, the Soviet Union, China, and perhaps India have been exceptions, but for the latter three security was by no means the sole incentive. Other states, such as Japan, Canada, Australia, and several European countries, with the technical skills and financial resources to build weapons have not felt strong incentives to do so and have refrained. Their alliances and available conventional weapons have enabled them to deal adequately with any serious threats to their security that they have perceived since World War II. The nuclear umbrella of the United States and to a lesser extent those of Britain and France have protected other NATO states and Japan; the Soviet Union has protected the Warsaw Pact states.

In contrast, the security disincentives for at least some of these states have been strong. Given their involvement in rather stable alliance systems, their dependence on American or Soviet goodwill, and their reluctance to stimulate others to go nuclear, Japanese, Australians, West Germans, Canadians, Italians, Swedes, Swiss, Czechs, Hungarians, and East Germans probably have calculated that nuclear weapons are more likely to decrease their security than to improve it. Unless current security arrangements in Europe and Asia begin to unravel, their assessments of their security will probably not change. Of course, incentives and disincentives of a nonsecurity nature also are important in determining the prospects for proliferation. For Britain, France, and India, for example, the decision to go nuclear was probably determined primarily by political rather than security interests.

For other governments, the security incentives in general seem stronger. Many of these states are involved in serious regional disputes or political competition. Few have the security of firm alliances with nuclear powers. Those that do seem increasingly less willing or able to rely on them. Several have experienced superpower intervention or have reason to fear it in the future. The fact that so few states have to date developed nuclear weapons is probably attributable to the strength of the security disincentives already discussed, the strength of other disincentives to be addressed below, and most nations' lack of capability thus far to build weapons. As these capabilities inevitably improve, compensating action will be required to strengthen disincentives and weaken incentives.

THREE

Political Objectives

Military power is a symbol and a source as well as an instrument of political power. The very existence of military forces can engender pride in a nation, enhance its prestige, and influence the psychological climate in which bargaining and negotiation are conducted. In the international arena in which conflicting interests and objectives of states are pursued, disputed, and frequently compromised short of war, military capability is one of any state's most useful assets. For these reasons nuclear incentives and disincentives must be sought in the political objectives of states no less than in their security objectives.

POLITICAL INCENTIVES

The foremost political incentive for acquiring nuclear weapons is their ability to enhance national power. They may not guarantee participation in the world's decision-making councils or the protection of a nation's regional and global interests, but in the absence of a coordinated policy to punish new nuclear states, they would certainly contribute. A new nuclear state could expect to increase over time its influence on regional security arrangements; in UN Security Council and General Assembly deliberations; and possibly even in such forums as the UN's specialized agencies, the International Energy Agency, and the UN Conference on the Law of the Sea. This new role would probably not develop rapidly or by conscious choice of other states. Instead it would be a rather natural and gradual result of the state's enhanced prestige and of subtle alterations in psychological orientation toward the new nuclear state. The translation of military power into political power may be gradual and complex, but it is nonetheless real. The more extensive the nuclear program, the greater its political significance.

States striving to achieve regional dominance or hegemony or to become global powers might view achievement of nuclear status as an essential milestone. Brazil, Zaire, Iran, and perhaps even Vietnam might be prompted to acquire nuclear weapons in order to enhance their regional importance. They would most likely succeed.

Globally, nuclear weapons seem a necessary but not sufficient requirement for guaranteeing that a state will participate in or be consulted about the resolution of major political and security disputes. Without nuclear weapons, Great Britain and France would have had greater difficulty in maintaining the special positions they have held in the world since World War II. China's acceptance as a global power derives in no small part (but certainly not entirely) from the size and growth of its nuclear arsenal. India has made no secret of its ambition to become a global power; its nuclear explosives program appears linked to this goal. To become a global power, however, requires more than just a few nuclear tests. A sizable nuclear arsenal, including regional- if not also continental-range delivery capability, must be acquired.

Another political incentive that may lead some states to develop nuclear weapons is global economic interests. Japan, West Germany, Canada, and to a lesser extent perhaps Sweden, Switzerland, and the Netherlands all have such interests but are not now striving to become global powers. They may acquiesce in their present position because they see their current political and diplomatic resources as sufficient to protect their interests. But their military alliances or shared interests with the United States may also contribute. They can rely on the United States, while acting on its own behalf, simultaneously to further some of their important interests. Without American support, at least some of these states would probably come to believe that they need global military power, including nuclear arms, to protect their global economic interests. In the future, other states that are unwilling or unable to rely on the United States or the Soviet Union for support may develop global economic interests. Such states may be more inclined than their present counterparts to protect those interests by acquiring nuclear weapons.

A nuclear weapons capability is a symbol of modernity and

technological competence as well as a source of status and prestige. In a world in which a few countries control most of the wealth, power, and expertise while the others struggle for economic independence and self-respect and occasionally fail to provide even food and shelter to their people, national leaders might see the acquisition of nuclear weapons as a relatively cheap and easy, but dramatic and useful, exercise of sovereignty. After all, the international inequalities imposed by the Non-Proliferation Treaty (NPT) system are among the few intended by design and agreement to be perpetual. A government might additionally hope that a nuclear weapons program would help it alleviate the frustrations of national poverty and economic and political development. Nuclear weapons might be expected to bolster a nation's self-confidence and prestige, to restore or strengthen popular support for a government, and to win respect from or even engender fear in neighbors, adversaries, and the world's great powers.

No one could pretend or expect that a nuclear explosion would either solve poor countries' economic and social problems or rapidly remove the basic inequity from the world's economic system. But resulting changes in attitude on the part of other states might be expected to yield some secondary benefits. Perhaps by coincidence, India's economic aid from Western industrial states was increased by some $200 million less than a month after its nuclear explosion. Such apparent linkages between nuclear capability and economic assistance will not be overlooked by other developing states.

Whatever economic or symbolic value may be gained by developing countries that achieve nuclear status will not easily be shared by other poor countries. In fact, other Third World countries are likely to experience a decline in security, relative power, and independence as they seek to adjust to the increased power of the new nuclear state. Only if a nuclear Third World state assertively tried, despite the cost to itself, to use its new power and prestige to advance a general redistribution of global wealth and power would any common benefit be forthcoming.

Some states might nonetheless see a different sort of nuclear incentive arising from the cleavage between the rich and poor countries. If the alliance of Third World countries continues to evolve into a strong global bargaining power, the benefits to be derived from leadership within it will correspondingly increase. A state aspiring to such a position might decide that in addition to becoming a vocal champion of

Third World causes, it must also achieve the prestige and respect given to nuclear powers. China's nuclear status appears to have so helped in its efforts to establish leadership in the Third World. India's explosion, in contrast, seems to have further eroded its claim to moral leadership among developing states. Iran, Mexico, Iraq, or Algeria—to name some of the nations currently aspiring to leadership roles—could draw either lesson from these experiences.

POLITICAL DISINCENTIVES

Several important political disincentives also influence states' decisions on whether to obtain nuclear weapons. The most significant is probably the widespread, but not universal, acceptance of the behavioral norm proscribing further proliferation that is embodied in the Non-Proliferation Treaty (NPT), the Treaty for the Prohibition of Nuclear Weapons in Latin America (Treaty of Tlatelolco), the safeguard system of the International Atomic Energy Agency (IAEA), and the efforts by states that manufacture nuclear reactors and other nuclear fuel-cycle facilities or components to agree on stricter controls and safeguards for exported equipment and technology. While not necessarily a decisive factor in any government's calculations of costs and benefits, this norm will act as an important restraining factor for all. Even India honored it in the breach by insisting that its test was not of a weapon but of a PNE.

A few states might exploit NPT or Treaty of Tlatelolco membership as a convenient deception to expedite access to nuclear materials and technology intended ultimately for weapons purposes. Such instances will be rare, however. International obligations such as these normally reflect the actual intentions of governments. Unless there is evidence to suggest the contrary, a country's acceptance of the NPT and safeguard restraints should be regarded as what it almost always is: a significant national undertaking, not easily revoked. The political commitments involved in their acceptance are as important as the accompanying physical constraints.

A decision by any country to develop nuclear weapons risks the condemnation and imposition of sanctions by international organizations and other states, whether allies or adversaries. The Soviet Union, for example, is unlikely to tolerate plans of a Warsaw Pact state to develop its own nuclear capability. Similarly, the hostile reactions of France, Britain, the Soviet Union, and perhaps the United States to a West German nuclear capability would probably damage West German political and economic interests more than a nuclear capability would aid them. The expectation or even the possibility of adverse reaction would have some damping effect on the nuclear desires of most governments. Allies and clients of the United States, including Australia, Israel, South Korea, and Taiwan, would have a particularly difficult task in assessing the risks of sanctions. The recent experience of Turkey demonstrated that Congress can effectively impose sanctions contrary to the wishes of the President and his advisers.

States would not always expect significant retaliation or condemnation, however. After all, with the possible exception of the termination of Soviet aid and subsequent Soviet hostility toward China, which in any case is not totally attributable to the Chinese nuclear decision, the first six nuclear states have not noticeably suffered from going nuclear. In particular, India, the most recent member of the nuclear club, seems on balance to have benefited despite some minor sanctions by Britain, Canada, Japan, and the United States. No international machinery or agreement exists to impose sanctions against a nuclear state. Except in special cases, economic sanctions are unlikely to be imposed by individual states or to work if tried. Sanctions against Rhodesia and South Africa, for example, have not been particularly effective. In short, although the norm proscribing further proliferation serves as an important moral and psychological impediment and can make the case of nuclear advocates in domestic debates seem much less attractive, it is unenforceable by any existing mechanism.

Just as a state might see its security interests threatened if its acquisition of nuclear weapons encouraged other states to do the same, so its political interests lie in not doing anything that would encourage its competitors to pursue a nuclear course. Both perceptions are likely to induce self-restraint. In fact, rarely would states want to encourage even their allies to achieve nuclear status. Any diffusion of nuclear weapons tends to dilute the advantage of those who already possess them. Moreover, alliances can change and dissolve, but nuclear weapons once acquired are likely to endure. Nevertheless, such long-term considerations may not be decisive for governments for which the planning horizon tends to be rather short.

53

Another important impediment to developing nuclear weapons has been the cost involved. As already pointed out, any state with a moderate level of industrialization could acquire in 5 to 15 years enough weapons material for at least a small number of crude nuclear explosives. The actual time required would depend on the extent of relevant prior training of technical personnel and on the overall level of industrialization of the country. The cost would be roughly tens of millions of dollars. While not a great deal of money for most countries to spend over a period of years, other military and development needs would always be competing for scarce resources. For many countries this competition would be so keen and other requirements for funds and technical personnel so great that the cost of a nuclear program would be a very significant disincentive.

In some countries, however, the extent of the economic and technical impediments to a nuclear weapons program will decline. The rise in oil prices since 1973 and the prevailing concern about future interruptions of oil supply for political purposes have increased interest in civilian nuclear electricity generation. Approximately 20 countries now operate power reactors, and some 15 more are building or have ordered their first. Many of these are Third World states. A significant number are not parties to the NPT. As civilian nuclear power industries mature, technical personnel receive training. Plutonium inventories in spent fuel or, if reprocessing facilities are available, in purified form build up. The lead time and cost involved in making weapons thereby decrease.

This decline of economic and technical barriers should not be overemphasized. Once weapons-grade material is acquired, weapons must still be produced and tested. Except for small-yield, inefficient devices tested in the atmosphere, this task is difficult and expensive. Most states would probably be reluctant to test in the atmosphere, whether because they are parties to the Partial Test Ban Treaty, do not have a convenient area under their control, or would prefer to avoid international condemnation for releasing radiation into the atmosphere. Moreover, many states would not initiate a nuclear explosives program just to produce a few cumbersome and inefficient weapons. They would want a true military capability that is secure, survivable, and under adequate control. The cost of building even a rather modest nuclear force would be close to or in excess of a billion dollars. The projection of costs of that magnitude would be an important disincentive to such states.

THE DOMESTIC POLITICAL PROCESS

Any country's decision to acquire nuclear weapons would be momentous. In most cases it would be made only after extensive debate, the nature of which would depend largely upon the type of political system combined with the psychological impact of world circumstances. In many countries the perceptions and opinions of a small and powerful elite or even of several key individuals will dominate. While people other than the decision makers would of course be required to carry out a nuclear program, the governments of certain of those countries would expect the necessary personnel either to see the wisdom of official policy or simply to follow orders. Even in countries with centralized and authoritarian political systems, however, participants in nuclear decision making or their advisers are likely to have differing interests and perspectives. Thus the process will probably include people who could argue the case for abstinence if they so chose. Whether in fact they would depends largely on their expectations of other participants in the process, their confidence in being persuasive, and the general psychological environment.

Diverse views may not always be represented, however. For example, a relatively small coalition of government officials and agencies were able to move France gradually toward nuclear weapons without prompting widespread concern or awareness within the government or among the public.[4] Wide debate did take place in France before the first test, but in countries with more authoritarian regimes and less democratic traditions there may be no chance for debate and dissent. Argentina's nuclear program currently seems to be proceeding in a manner not too dissimilar from that of France in the 1950s.

Whether or not differing perspectives are represented in the debate, in countries with elite decision making the general public may not even learn about the program until after a first test and then may or may not be free to express its opinions. In the Soviet Union, in the People's Republic of China and, because of special wartime conditions, also in the United States, the initial nuclear program was secret. Whether a nuclear program would bring support or opposition to the regime depends on

[4]Lawrence Scheinmann, *Atomic Energy Policy in France under the Fourth Republic*, Princeton University Press, Princeton, N.J., 1965.

unique circumstances. In India, for instance, a small number of government officials, bureaucrats, and scientists decided on and implemented the nuclear program. Public announcement following the first test brought wide popular acclaim.

Several states could be expected to have wider public participation in nuclear decision making and to be more influenced by public attitudes. Japan, Sweden, and Australia have had public debates on nuclear weapons. Internationally oriented segments of the public would probably be influenced by their expectation of other states' reactions and intentions as well as by their perception of the strength of the international norm against proliferation. Traditionally nationalistic, chauvinistic, and expansionist elements would probably support a nuclear program. Industrial, commercial, and economic development interests are likely to be wary of the diversion of needed resources and to fear damaging economic reprisals, but might still believe that the long-term political or military benefits from going nuclear would outweigh the immediate disadvantages. The military might favor a nuclear program as a means of extending its own power and importance, oppose it as a detrimental provocation to adversaries and a drain on resources needed for other military purposes, or split into two camps. The scientific community might be similarly divided. Its dominant considerations are likely to be nonscientific, even though a nuclear program would directly affect the extent and emphasis of government support for science and technology. Obviously the likely outcome of public debate cannot be specified in general, but would depend on unique features of each country. Informed speculation would require a detailed, country-specific analysis.

For any sort of decision-making process, the significance of the psychological environment and global events cannot be overemphasized. A strong international norm against proliferation accompanied by a sense that acquisition of nuclear weapons by neighbors, adversaries, or simply many other countries was not inevitable would strengthen the position of nuclear opponents. If the norm were weakened and proliferation seemed inevitable, their case would be harder to sustain. The psychological impact of multiple withdrawals from the NPT or of near-simultaneous nuclear acquisition by several states could result in a snowballing effect.

FOUR

Reducing Incentives and Increasing Disincentives

Many means have been suggested to reduce states' incentives or increase their disincentives to obtain nuclear weapons. They range from extending superpower security guarantees to implementing superpower arms control, from manipulating symbols to initiating massive transfers of wealth and power, from regional security arrangements to economic and military sanctions. Many of the usual proposals, however, do not reflect an understanding of which nuclear incentives are most important. Most proposals conflict with important goals in other policy areas. Some simply seem so unlikely to be effective as not to merit the great effort their adoption would require. Identifying approaches that avoid these faults is difficult, particularly since, despite some similarities, each state's motivations are unique.

REDUCING SECURITY INCENTIVES

The dominant nuclear incentive for many states is the requirement to protect their security. Reducing this incentive requires providing non-nuclear substitutes. Formerly the most important alternatives were an alliance with and security guarantees from one of the superpowers, usually the United States. The success of these arrangements has been less than total. Neither the NATO alliance nor American nuclear guarantees prevented the United Kingdom and France from developing their own nuclear forces. Nonetheless, American security treaties have provided Western European states, Japan, Taiwan, South Korea, and

Australia with assurances that the prestige, wealth, power, and, if necessary, nuclear arsenal of the United States would protect their security. While the credibility of these guarantees has fluctuated, they have been and still are important instruments for reducing these states' incentives to follow an independent nuclear path to their security.

As a straightforward extrapolation of past successes, an extension of superpower guarantees to additional potential proliferants seems an obvious way to decrease security incentives for nuclear acquisition. There are a number of difficulties with this approach, however. First, the security guarantees might have to be directed against other allies of the prospective guarantor, states with which the guarantor would wish to maintain stable relations, or potential proliferants themselves. Unless adversaries of the guaranteed state would acquiesce to the security arrangement, they would probably interpret the extension of the guarantee as a hostile act, thereby contributing to their own incentives to acquire nuclear weapons.

Second, the potential guarantors are naturally reluctant to extend security guarantees. Formal guarantees or alliances, if they are to be at all meaningful, cannot be extended lightly and must have implications beyond the security realm. They involve broad political and frequently economic as well as military commitments. They suggest that the guarantor sees the future of the guaranteed state as important and imply its willingness to assist politically and economically in areas not specifically covered by the terms of the security guarantees. They imply acceptance not only of the state's sovereignty and of the inviolability of its borders, but also of the legitimacy of its present regime.

The extension of security guarantees therefore implies that the guarantor either is willing to become a partial hostage and party to the domestic and foreign policies of another government or is prepared to exert some control over those policies. For the foreseeable future, the United States seems likely to be very reluctant to entwine itself in that way through new commitments. In a few special cases—perhaps Israel, Egypt, and other Arab states in the context of an overall Middle East settlement—American security guarantees might be negotiable. But an antiproliferation policy that counted on expanding American security guarantees as a main pillar is bound to fail, at least in the near term. A formal guarantee to South Africa is unlikely, for example, because it would suggest that the United States accepted the present government and its policy of apartheid and would thereby damage American relations with black Africa and the rest of the Third World.

The third difficulty with extending guarantees is the obverse of the second. Acceptance of security guarantees implies a willingness by the guaranteed state to let the guarantor influence aspects of its foreign and domestic policy. Many states would be unwilling to accept these conditions.

Finally, security guarantees are difficult to make credible enough that a guaranteed state would be willing to forego what it might otherwise consider a central pillar of its own foreign and military policy. Credibility comes not from signatures on a formal document but from perceptions of strong and enduring common interest, a guarantor's record of honoring commitments, and, at least for the United States, a perception of widespread popular and congressional support for the government guaranteed. At least for the immediate future, the United States' ability to extend new credible guarantees is severely limited.

Indeed, maintaining the credibility of even existing American commitments will be difficult. Several potential nuclear states—including Japan, Taiwan, South Korea, Australia, Iran, Pakistan, Israel, and Western European countries—are American allies or clients. To the extent that national security needs may provoke them to acquire nuclear weapons, their perceptions of the strength and steadfastness of American commitments will be critical to their nuclear choices and occasionally decisive. Of course, this fact in itself is not sufficient reason to conclude that the United States must prevent the weakening of its guarantees. Other, frequently competing objectives must generally be weighted in such decisions. The point here is simply to stress that the continued credibility of American security guarantees is likely to affect the security incentives of potential nuclear states.

Over the longer term there may be new possibilities for relying on extended security guarantees. While the United States is retrenching its foreign commitments, the Soviet Union, perhaps stimulated by a perception of American reluctance to compete, is now increasingly active in many countries and regions. It is not inconceivable that over the next 10 to 15 years, the Soviets will develop bilateral relationships that will reduce countries' incentives to acquire nuclear weapons.

The international involvement of the United States might decline over the next 10 years or, perhaps stimulated by a more assertive Soviet foreign policy, it might increase. A trend toward renewed great-power competition could lead to greater popular and official support in the United States for strengthening and extending its alliance system. This may be viewed as good or bad, depending on ideology and judgments about the outcome and that of alternative futures. In any case, such a renewed confrontation would probably increase the credibility of American guarantees and thus reduce many states' security incentives to go nuclear. Some, of course, would prefer to remain aloof from the superpower alliance system. For them, a period of greater global competition might induce more insecurity and therefore increased need for nuclear weapons.

If this trend toward greater superpower competition should in fact develop, it could result in a renewed emphasis on strong alliances, perhaps expanding to embrace regions previously outside or on the edge of the East-West confrontation. Ultimately the result might be a world divided into competing spheres of influence of the great powers. The leaders—the United States, the Soviet Union, and conceivably China—could remain in confrontation by trying constantly to alter the boundaries of influence to their own advantage, or they could tacitly agree to refrain from interfering in the regions dominated and kept peaceful by the others. Neither of these scenarios seems likely since each would require a reversal of the recent drift toward a more multipolar international system. They nonetheless are not inconceivable. The international structure they imply would be coercive and inflexible, with power relationships largely frozen and the nationalistic and economic aspirations of much of the world's population frustrated. It would also be one in which the incentives and even the opportunities for proliferation would be largely absent. However, its costs are too high to make it a desirable solution to the proliferation problem.

Another non-nuclear alternative is conventional arms. States sufficiently armed with such weapons to be confident of their ability to deter or protect themselves against potential aggressors will have less reason to acquire nuclear weapons. But since most states lack either or both the financial resources and technical capability to satisfy their perceived needs for conventional weapons by domestic production, they must purchase arms from the major industrial states.

Offering weapons alone on a commercial basis may not be sufficient, though, even if they are the most modern weapons. Many countries will need or want, in addition to the hardware, financial assistance for their purchases, manpower training in the use and maintenance of the equipment, assistance with building airports or other military facilities, logistical support and guarantees for the supply of spare parts, and given the high rates of equipment consumption in modern warfare, promises of resupply in wartime. These are the sorts of services that the United States now provides Israel, Saudi Arabia, Iran, and others.

Any decision to furnish extensive supplies of conventional arms will be made on the basis of broad considerations. Among others is the possibility that large arms transfers to one state may encourage its adversary to go nuclear. Requests for modern precision-guided munitions in particular, even when coming from traditional recipients of large arms sales or transfers, will raise difficult political and military issues for suppliers. The argument here is not for a permissive policy of arms transfers. The regulation or control of the arms trade is a complex and important issue that cannot be addressed within this essay's scope. Rather, it is intended merely to point out that denying requests for weapons or attaching excessive financial or political prices might reinforce *some* domestic elements that seek independence, security, power, or budgetary savings through nuclear weapons. Pakistan's Prime Minister, for example, has said that a sure supply of conventional arms from the United States might preclude his country's having to respond to India's explosion with a nuclear weapons program of its own. (Since Pakistan has wanted a greater supply of American weapons for many years, however, this somewhat ambiguous statement was self-serving whether a serious threat or not.) Particularly for countries such as Israel, South Africa, South Korea, and Taiwan, where sovereignty or regimes are under challenge, the goal of nonproliferation may come into direct conflict with the objective of reducing arms transfers.

The contrary may also be true in some cases, however. Assisting a state to buttress its military forces and thereby increasing its power and ambition might strengthen those domestic elements favoring a nuclear weapons capability. At best the issue is ambiguous and indeterminant.

To assuage those unaligned non-nuclear states fearful of nuclear attack, an effort might be made to reduce or counterbalance the nuclear threat or to extend nuclear protection. Some steps have already been taken. In 1964, after China exploded its first nuclear weapons, President Johnson promised American support to any country coming under the threat of Chinese blackmail. China has now given the same pledge to any state that is the object of an Indian nuclear attack. UN Security Council Resolution 255 (June 1968) has a similar aim. It states that "aggression with nuclear weapons or the threat of such aggression against a non-nuclear-weapon state would create a situation in which the Security Council and above all its nuclear-weapon state permanent members, would have to act immediately in accordance with their obligations under the United Nations Charter." Neither unilateral statements nor multilateral resolutions that are subject to veto, however, are likely to be either credible or useful unless they are integral components of a more general alliance or collective security system.

A public declaration by nuclear weapons states, separately or collectively, that they would not use or threaten to use nuclear weapons against non-nuclear states—or, in a weaker form, against non-nuclear states that are not supported by another nuclear weapons state—would be another approach to the same problem.[5] Such a declaration might allay the concerns of those states for which the fear of nuclear attack and coercion is an especially salient nuclear incentive and undermine the arguments of their nuclear proponents. It might also have some utility in the context of nuclear-free zones, as discussed below. But even in these cases, the overall status of particular bilateral relationships would have a more significant influence on nations' perceptions of their security than would pious assurances. The threat to employ nuclear weapons must inevitably exist as long as nuclear weapons do. Non-nuclear states fearing nuclear attack are unlikely to be mollified by a declaration of restraint, no matter how solemn. The threat, unstated before the declaration no less than after, would still persist. More important, governments are usually more concerned about neighboring states than distant nuclear powers. When they do perceive threats from nuclear powers, they are normally most worried about conventional, not nuclear, attack. A no-use declaration would not address these more important security problems. By decreasing the apparent significance of nuclear weapons in relations between states, a no-use-against-non-nuclear-states declaration might have sym-

---

[5]No first use against any state is still another possibility that might be considered. Since such a proposal is not likely to have any greater impact on security incentives, discussion is deferred to the subsequent section on reducing political incentives.

bolic and political importance in reducing proliferation incentives, but it is unlikely to be important from a security perspective.[6]

In fact, it might even be counterproductive. If the declaration's wording did not explicitly rule out its application to North Korea, for example, South Korea might well react by commencing a nuclear weapons program—not because nuclear weapons would be necessary or particularly useful for its own defense, but because the presence of tactical nuclear weapons in South Korea and the United States' official willingness to use them in that country's defense are fundamental to the credibility of the American security guarantee. An American no-use declaration would almost certainly be interpreted as signaling a reduced willingness to stand by its treaty commitment to South Korea. The exclusion of North Korea could be assured if the declaration were limited to non-nuclear states neither allied with nor receiving assistance from nuclear powers. In any case, the United States would almost certainly have to accompany a no-use-against-non-nuclear-states declaration with strong reassurances not only to South Korea but also to other states whose confidence in its guarantees might be undermined, including Taiwan, Japan, Australia, and particularly Western European countries.

Another approach to reducing security-related nuclear incentives would be a regional security agreement that eliminated nuclear weapons from a region.[7] Even if such a nuclear-free zone were no more than a joint enunciation by states of their own intentions not to acquire nuclear weapons, it would still have some attractiveness as an extension of the NPT. Since states are frequently encouraged to acquire nuclear weapons, or at least to keep open the option, by fear that other regional states will themselves do so, a combined renunciation of nuclear capability might be possible even though a series of unilateral actions were not. In addition, such a regional agreement would strengthen the norm against acquiring nuclear weapons by applying it locally. This proximity

[6]For a different view of no-use and no-first-use declarations see Richard H. Ullman, "No First Use of Nuclear Weapons," *Foreign Affairs,* vol. 50, no. 4 (July 1972), pp. 669–683.

[7]A particularly useful discussion of nuclear-free zones is provided in the rapporteur's report, entitled "Nuclear-Weapon-Free Zones," of a conference sponsored by the Stanley Foundation, October 7–9, 1975.

would have a more powerful effect on regional states than would the NPT itself.

However, nuclear-free-zone proposals usually go beyond the provisions of the NPT. They are normally assumed to include prohibitions against regional deployment of nuclear weapons even if under the control of outside states, no-use assurances by nuclear states, and sometimes a ban against transit of nuclear weapons through the designated region. These extensions are both a strength and a weakness. If agreed to by nonregional nuclear powers, such assurances, to the limited extent that they would reduce states' security worries, would provide additional incentives to participate. But they would frequently challenge existing security relationships and thus might alienate important regional states and external nuclear powers. (Indeed, to some proponents the challenge to the status quo is one of the important purposes of proposals such as that for an Indian Ocean Zone of Peace.) In these cases, the extensions would make agreement more difficult or in fact prevent the achievement of what would be, even without such troublesome aspects, a useful instrument to reduce security incentives. Nuclear-free-zone proposals for the Nordic area, for example, would falter on any stipulation that interfered with American nuclear commitments to its NATO allies. An Indian Ocean or Oceania nuclear-free zone would not receive superpower support if it restricted transport. Although some states would clearly prefer such extensions to be included in a nuclear-free-zone agreement, they do not seem central to the agreements' value as nonproliferation instruments. More progress might be possible were more limited objectives adopted.

If nuclear-free-zone proposals are to be implemented, they require states that may well be bitter opponents or political competitors to agree on fundamental security matters. In the Middle East and southern Asia, for example, it seems unlikely that a nuclear-free-zone agreement could precede a resolution of serious regional security issues. States are not likely to forego nuclear weapons, potentially their most important instrument of power, until all regional disputes are settled or so frozen that change cannot reasonably be expected or until a regional mechanism for the settlement of disputes has gained acceptance. Certainly some states in a volatile region may conclude that a general foreswearing of the nuclear option would be most in their interests, but the likelihood that all others would share this attitude seems small. Many would not want to renounce the advantages to be gained through subtle hints. Where outstanding regional disputes do exist, attempts to resolve them, reliance on the more internationally oriented Non-Proliferation Treaty, and perhaps extension of superpower security guarantees would probably be more fruitful than immediate efforts to establish nuclear-free zones.

There are some regions, however, where nuclear-free zones, perhaps in the limited form proposed above, might actually be feasible as well as useful. The Latin America free-zone agreement, for example, is in effect in almost all Latin American countries. It would be more significant if Argentina, Brazil, and Cuba were full parties. But Argentina and Brazil have signed and Brazil has ratified without the required declaration of waiver to bring it into force. As a formal enunciation of a norm of acceptable behavior, the treaty renders the political decision by any Latin American state to initiate a nuclear weapons program very difficult.

Africa would be another interesting case to examine—particularly sub-Sahara Africa in order to avoid the requirement of first settling the Middle East conflict. There would be difficulties in getting these frequently disputatious states to agree on a matter of overriding general interest, but with time and the efforts of a creative and resourceful advocate these might be overcome. South Africa would cause serious problems: first, it is the African state closest to nuclear status and might be unwilling to join; second, other states might not want to give the current regime legitimacy by including it in negotiations and in the ultimate agreement. Proceeding on such an agreement without South Africa would still be valuable and might be more feasible if superpower guarantees were incorporated. In any case, progress would be slow and difficult.

Another region where a nuclear-free zone might succeed if the difficult problem of transit of nuclear weapons through the region were avoided is the Oceania area that includes Malaysia, Singapore, Indonesia, the Philippines, Australia, New Zealand, and the smaller islands. Actually, any arrangement that included Australia and Indonesia would be useful.

REDUCING POLITICAL INCENTIVES

Superpower arms control is frequently said to be an important instrument for reducing states' incentives to go nuclear. Yet the major security problem of non-nuclear (including those in Europe) with respect to nuclear states is to deter or defend against conventional incursion and coercion, not nuclear attack. Superpower arms control will therefore have no impact on the security incentives for proliferation. Weapons reductions are also unlikely to be anywhere near large enough actually to reduce the power of the United States and Soviet Union relative to non-nuclear states. Therefore whether outcomes of SALT or of other unilateral or bilateral processes, superpower arms control agreements will be effective primarily as political symbols. This symbolism is important, but less so than is frequently claimed.[8] Reductions in the superpowers' strategic or tactical nuclear weapons or restrictions on research and development would create the appearance that nuclear weapons are a declining political asset. By symbolizing the superpowers' willingness to forgo important sources of power, just as non-nuclear NPT signatories have done, they would also make the inequities of the NPT appear less significant.

At least for some non-nuclear states, a comprehensive test ban is a particularly important symbol of their efforts to constrain the power of nuclear states. Yet these perceptions are unfounded. A complete cessation of testing would not actually decrease the power of the United States and the Soviet Union. Indeed, since the most vociferous non-nuclear proponents of a comprehensive test ban are unlikely to develop their own weapons, it is questionable whether such a treaty would have any effect at all on nuclear proliferation. If it did, it would derive almost exclusively from the participation of the United States and the Soviet Union. Its contribution would therefore not depend on universal adherence.

A Threshold Test Ban Treaty (TTBT) of the sort now pending between the United States and Soviet Union, while not going as far toward a comprehensive test ban as many people would like, nonetheless seems

[8] A different view of the importance of superpower nuclear arms control is presented in William Epstein, *The Last Chance: Nuclear Proliferation and Arms Control*, The Free Press, New York, 1976.

beneficial in the Soviet-American context. But this is not a judgment about its utility as an instrument of nonproliferation policy. Certainly the fact of the accord itself will have some symbolic value. More important, however, by explicitly permitting relatively small nuclear weapons to be tested, the TTBT seems to make them legitimate and even highlights their military, political, and symbolic significance. Any state's initial nuclear explosion will be small, certainly below the 150-kiloton threshold. Moreover, the TTBT, like the NPT, reinforces and reemphasizes the legitimacy and economic value of PNEs by dealing with them in a special agreement, even though specifying the same threshold yield. Therefore states wanting to test a nuclear device and minimize subsequent reprobation might be encouraged to exploit—as did India—the convenient PNE excuse. They might even be encouraged to develop nuclear explosives solely for their economic benefit. But given the great expense of such a program, the declining enthusiasm for PNEs in the United States,[9] and the refusal of most countries to recognize a distinction betweeen peaceful explosions and weapons, such an innocent PNE program seems very unlikely. On balance, then, the Threshold Test Ban Treaty probably is marginally counterproductive in its effect on impeding nuclear proliferation.

The Non-Proliferation Treaty requires that nuclear weapons states provide peaceful nuclear technology, including the benefits of peaceful nuclear explosions, to nonweapon states. As no mechanism has yet been established to provide for the PNE aspects of this mandate, the supposed shirking of obligation by nuclear weapons states is sometimes said to stimulate proliferation. Actually there is no reason to think that this is the case. Despite occasional interest and studies, no non-nuclear state has ever officially requested PNE services. Thus the potential providers are not in technical violation of their obligations. The important question, however, is not a legalistic one. Either nuclear states can maintain a low-profile skepticism toward the utility of PNEs without foreclosing the possibility of offering assistance if asked or they can establish a

[9]See Gulf Universities Research Consortium, *PNE (Peaceful Nuclear Explosion) Activity Projections for Arms Control Planning, ACDA-/PAB-253*, April 1975, and *An Analysis of the Economic Feasibility, Technical Significance and Time Scale for Application of Peaceful Nuclear Explosions in the U.S., with special reference to the GURC Report thereon*, final report to the U.S. Arms Control and Disarmament Agency from the Program on Science, Technology and Society, Cornell University, April 1975.

formal mechanism to provide PNEs and thereby probably stimulate widespread interest. Of these choices, the former seems preferable. Since the goal is to plug both the real and symbolic aspects of the PNE loophole, subtle suppression that leaves open the option of formal renunciation is better than enthusiastic or even modest marketing.

In this connection, it is worth mentioning that the United States government accepts India's disclaimer of weapons intentions. This is a prudent stance insofar as the United States wants to maintain disincentives against India's developing nuclear weapons systems. Indeed, to the extent that private or official commentators on the Indian explosion emphasize the distance between a single or small number of explosions and a significant military capability, the value of the Indian test will seem to (and therefore really will) diminish. While this policy of not challenging the PNE claim reduces its perceived value—prestige and strategic—and therefore the incentive for other states to follow suit, tacit acceptance at the same time undermines the normative barriers against nuclear tests disguised as PNEs. Here again, important objectives are in direct conflict. Pursuing either policy option simultaneously strengthens both incentives and disincentives.

As already suggested, declaration of nonuse of nuclear weapons against non-nuclear states would have some utility in reducing the apparent significance of nuclear weapons in international politics. There is a still stronger form of nonuse assurance: a blanket pledge, of the sort the Chinese affirm, never to be the first to use nuclear weapons. Such a declaration might impede proliferation through its suggestion that governments do not believe an overt threat to employ nuclear weapons serves useful political and diplomatic purposes.

The major difficulty with such a no-first-use policy is that nuclear weapons do in fact serve useful political and diplomatic functions. The nuclear uncertainty facing any potential aggressor in Europe, or for that matter in Asia, is an important part of deterrence policy. Moreover, an American no-first-use declaration would undermine the credibility of its political and security commitments, which would be a high price to pay. It certainly should not be paid without what is, for the foreseeable future, the rather unlikely concurrence of the United States' European and Asian allies or without a high likelihood that the pledge would actually contribute significantly to inhibiting proliferation. Since its effect would be primarily symbolic, there is certainly no such assurance. Indeed, by weakening the credibility of American guarantees, the net effect of such a declaration might be to stimulate proliferation. On balance therefore, a no-first-use pledge is not a useful component of a nonproliferation strategy.

Any arms control efforts—whether strategic arms limitations, nuclear test bans, or no-first-use declarations—are unlikely to inhibit proliferation significantly unless they result from a process of negotiations and institution or regime building. One or more unilateral declarations, adopted as isolated acts of magnanimity, would not signal a significant change in world security arrangements and therefore would probably be ineffective. It is the promise of substantial change, even if symbolic, that is the important political and psychological aspect of any arms control actions (short of almost total nuclear disarmament). Such a promise can only be attained through policy review, negotiation, and institution building.

Declaratory statements by nuclear powers also influence proliferation incentives by signaling others about their views on the importance and utility of nuclear weapons. It is therefore important to ask how declaratory statements might be used to reduce other nations' motivations to go nuclear. (Nuclear saber rattling, nuclear force deployments, and annual budgetary appropriations also convey relevant signals but are less amenable to conscious manipulation for the purpose of influencing nuclear incentives of others.) Given the political systems and budgetary processes in other nuclear states and the resultant dearth of publicized official statements about nuclear weapons, this discussion must focus on the United States.

There are three impediments to progress. First, because of the nature of the American political system, nuclear weapons are frequently discussed in public by American governmental officials. Their importance cannot therefore be deemphasized, as it could in other countries, simply by lack of public attention. Second, since almost all of these leaders in fact believe that nuclear arsenals are valuable assets in the conduct of foreign policy, they would have difficulty pretending otherwise in their public statements. Third, American officials must address diverse audiences. They must annually argue their case for budgetary appropriations before Congress and the American public; in doing so, they must both stress the value of nuclear weapons and discuss matters of targeting and technical detail that are rarely examined openly in other countries. This approach inevitably signals to others the importance that the United States attributes to its nuclear capacities. Officials must persuade allies of the strength and steadfastness of American support and discuss the role that nuclear weapons play in guaranteeing their security. Moreover, to assure that the nuclear deterrent remains credible, they must also convey to current and potential opponents the ability and especially the will to use nuclear weapons if necessary.

While signaling these various intents, it is very difficult to convey simultaneously to non-nuclear states, who inevitably listen in, that nuclear weapons really are not so important and that those who do not have them should consider themselves fortunate. But it should not be totally impossible. Public declarations are weighed and discounted according to their source and the forums in which they are delivered. Most important is that government officials recognize that potential proliferants listen to and are influenced by what is said. Simply tempering language and altering nuances could change the messages received by non-nuclear states.

Other actions could be taken by the international community to decrease the symbolic importance of nuclear weapons. Despite the inevitable psychological impact of a state's first nuclear explosion, other states should adopt a calculated policy designed to deny or minimize the visible signs of enhanced prestige to the new nuclear state. Nothing should be done to recognize an increase in status. Instead the response should be reprobation for having violated an important international behavioral norm and for having threatened international peace and security.

Alternative means should also be developed for Third World states to increase their prestige, exercise their sovereignty, and demonstrate their equality with others. An invitation to Japan to become a permanent member of the UN Security Council, though unlikely, would suggest that possession of nuclear weapons is not the only criterion for being considered a preeminent country. Providing a permanent seat to India, of course, would have precisely the opposite effect. Offering greater access to, participation in, and power to influence such international decision-making bodies as the International Monetary Fund or the International Atomic Energy Agency might transform other assets—be they wealth, oil, or technological sophistication—into symbols as significant as nuclear weapons. Official American recognition of the special status of Brazil in South America is a move in this direction.

The management of the international nuclear industry is particularly significant for proliferation because of its close relationship to nuclear weapons capabilities. Internationalization of important aspects of the fuel cycle has been proposed as a means of reducing discrimination against non-nuclear states. Nuclear states should also consider submitting their nonmilitary nuclear facilities to international safeguards requirements in order to eliminate one of the most important symbolic inequalities of the NPT system. If a nuclear supplier's agreement is to avoid reinforcing the perception of power disparity between nuclear and non-nuclear states, it should be ratified and managed by the world community, perhaps using the mechanism of the IAEA governing board. Indeed, a buyers' agreement or a joint suppliers'-buyers' agreement would be preferable, as will be detailed below.

Reducing the real, as opposed to the symbolic, power of nuclear weapons is more difficult. In fact, that power probably cannot be decreased any more than a state's possession of army divisions, naval ships, or a bomber force can somehow be made irrelevant to its real or perceived power. A more useful exercise would be to devise ways of obviating states' needs to increase their power by acquiring nuclear weapons. Other than by making nuclear weapons seem irrelevant, in a symbolic sense, to nations' political objectives, the only other way to reduce the saliency of political goals that act as nuclear incentives is to fulfill or begin to fulfill them. This strategy raises the difficult issue of the ability of governments to use the threat of going nuclear for coercion or blackmail.

Non-nuclear states are unlikely to attempt coercion or blackmail by overtly threatening to go nuclear. Such a threat made against a neighboring state (to settle territorial or other disputes) would be equivalent to or more serious than a threat to employ conventional military force. It would probably be rejected and could, if both parties were capable of obtaining nuclear weapons, stimulate a nuclear arms race in the area. Open conventional warfare or other sorts of threats are more likely to be successful. A threat to go nuclear would be no more successful against one or both superpowers or even against the industrialized states in general. No matter how justified the threatening state's objectives, an overt nuclear threat is unlikely to attain its ends. If it were allowed to, states could become liable to nuclear blackmail in the process of preventing proliferation.

Threats can be made which are not explicit. The subtle, gradual, but relentless threats are likely to be the most effective and will raise the greatest problem for the superpowers and the world community. The most credible means of exerting this sort of threat is a gradual development of a nuclear power industry or, as Israel has done, a nuclear research program that shortens the lead time from a decision to acquire nuclear weapons to accomplishment. Argentina, Brazil, Iran, South Africa, South Korea, and Taiwan are all acquiring a nuclear industry that will improve their capabilities to produce nuclear weapons and provide them with the opportunity to manipulate subtly the threat to do so. Israel has been skillfully extracting political benefit from its near-nuclear status for years. India played the same game for some time but finally cashed the first chip. Its game is by no means over, however; attention is now focused on the size, scope, and purpose of the future test program. To the extent that states develop a credible capability to go nuclear quickly, other states can be expected to treat them in ways calculated to dissuade them from doing so. This may sometimes involve threat and sanction, but it may also lead to the achievement of real benefit.

Subtle threats involve the risk of blackmail no less than overt threats do. Nevertheless, some of the ambitions of near-nuclear states must inevitably be partially satisfied as an aspect of any nonproliferation strategy. When those objectives would be supported anyway for reasons totally unrelated to nuclear weapons, this would not be difficult. The United States would undoubtedly accommodate Iran's regional ambitions, protect Japan's global economic interests, and act to guarantee Israel's existence even in the absence of an implied threat to go nuclear. But should the United States and others support the ambitions of Brazil, Argentina, and India or the security of South Africa? If so, how far and at the expense of which of their own competing objectives and those of other states? What about Nigeria, Zaire, Vietnam, or other states that may pursue hegemonial interests in the future? These questions can be answered only on a case-by-case basis.

In many instances, the threat to go nuclear will not just be inexplicit and subtle but also latent. Many Third World countries are so far from a nuclear capability that no threats are credible. But in the 1980s this analysis may change, particularly for those states whose economic prospects could improve. Some may aspire to regional or Third World leadership, but most will remain concerned primarily with the equality of nations and world redistribution of wealth and power. Some observers have suggested the utility of striking a global bargain in which the poor willingly forgo nuclear weapons and the rich give up a portion of their wealth and prerogative. Industrialized states could, for example, tie increases in foreign aid, technology transfer, or trading preferences for poor countries to participation in the NPT. Creating an institutional framework would not be easy, given the coordination problems within and among governments across quite disconnected policy areas. Even without these problems, there would still be serious difficulties. The industrialized states could see the bargain as nuclear blackmail. Many Third World states might resent its patronizing implications and see the whole effort as an unwarranted interference in their national sovereignty by the industrialized world; worse yet, they might view the level of benefits, no matter how large, as evidence that the rich were continuing their policy of domination and neocolonialism with only enough scraps thrown to the poor to keep them from starving outright. Moreover, a significant transfer of wealth would be permanent, while promises related to nuclear abstinence could be broken.

The same objectives may be better served without a global bargain of this sort. Redistribution of the world's wealth need not be tied to a nonproliferation policy. Mechanisms already exist that could accomplish that objective. The United Nations or the Organization for Economic Cooperation and Development could accomplish the task. The OPEC countries, or at least those whose income far surpasses their domestic monetary requirements, could transform themselves (to use an American analogy) into a combined Internal Revenue Service and Health, Education and Welfare Department for the world. None of these things is likely to happen. The problem is not the lack of mechanisms, but the lack of will. And the latent or implicit threat of proliferation is not likely to increase that will substantially. There may be many reasons why a redistribution of wealth, technology, and economic power should be initiated, but it should and can best be done without explicit linkages to proliferation.

Indeed, any effort to support the objectives or redress the grievances of states in order to reduce their nuclear incentives might actually be counterproductive. To the extent that states' hegemonial or leadership ambitions are satisfied, their desires for a stable and growing stake in the world economy fulfilled, or their appetites for a larger share of the world's wealth whetted, their incentives for obtaining nuclear weapons might rise. So long as sufficient progress is made, they may be content to bide their time. But if the momentum dissipates, obstacles appear, or the need for self-reliance to protect their gains is recognized, governments may see nuclear weapons as a logical and important instrument of national purpose. Moreover, as a government achieves its political and economic objectives, a state's technical and industrial base, its economy's ability to sustain a weapons program, and in all probability, its access to fissile material will increase. While a decision not to build a nuclear weapon can always be revoked at some economic and political cost, the physical construction capacity can only increase with time, and the political and security incentives might do so in parallel.

INCREASING DISINCENTIVES

Increasing disincentives means raising the perceived costs of going nuclear, whether in terms of security, power, or wealth. By promising assistance to non-nuclear states that come under nuclear threat or attack, Security Council Resolution 255, to the extent that it is credible, would deter the use of nuclear weapons and therefore, to a small extent, also deter their acquisition. But to be really effective in inhibiting proliferation, threats should be directed against the development of nuclear weapons rather than their use.

If threats are really to inhibit proliferation, they should be directed against the development of nuclear weapons rather than their use. One obvious approach would be for one or both superpowers to threaten to seize or destroy nuclear materials, facilities, and weapons in any newly nuclear country. The threatened intervention could be nuclear, conventional, or unspecified. But such an approach would not be useful. Since non-nuclear states would regard this policy as egregious imperialism or a superpower condominium, the political cost would be high. Moreover, the threat to intervene would not be credible. When the time came to make it good, the chances of Soviet-American agreement and joint action would be small. Intervention by one superpower could lead to extended and unwanted warfare and might involve military confrontation with the other. Finally, the effects of an intervention would be temporary unless the invading power intended to control important aspects of the country's domestic and foreign policy from then on. Such a policy therefore would be costly, hollow, and fraught with risks.

Another potential threat is an announcement by the United States or the Soviet Union of a policy of targeting, not necessarily with nuclear weapons, all nuclear weapons facilities—including storage depots, weapons fabrication plants, and fissile-material production plants—of new nuclear countries. This approach is totally different from threatening intervention to destroy facilities. While it would probably be credible, its effect as a nuclear disincentive is likely to be minimal. Any prudent government would always assume that its important military sites already were or could rapidly be targeted by the superpowers' long-range delivery systems. But military forces that are targeted and not used are benign, except to the extent that the announcement of a targeting policy would exert coercive psychological pressure. Although an explicit threat of this sort would exert such pressure, it would probably be insufficient to influence significantly a state's evaluation of its nuclear option. It would, however, almost certainly lead to condemnation of the threatening superpower and an erosion of its political position in the Third World. On balance, it would probably be counterproductive.

A somewhat altered version of Security Council Resolution 255, which focused not on nuclear use or threat but on acquisition itself, should be considered. Even if, as seems probable, there would be no associated sanction other than a required Security Council debate, the resolution itself would be a useful symbolic expression of concern by the international community. Even a Soviet-American declaration stating that acquisition of nuclear weapons was a serious threat to world peace and security and would result in their consulting about the possibility of joint action would have some utility. Because of its implications of superpower condominium, however, it would elicit opposition from many quarters. Both the bilateral and Security Council proposals have a further drawback. While they may serve as disincentives before the next state goes nuclear, if they failed to prevent further proliferation, the absence of any real security sanctions would be highlighted and the disincentives for other potential proliferants thereby reduced.

A variation of the proposal recently made by Alton Frye[10] might, in some limited circumstances, be useful. A superpower or other nuclear

---

[10]Alton Frye, "How to Ban the Bomb: Sell It," *The New York Times Magazine*, January 11, 1976.

state could inform or merely hint to its allies' adversaries or potential adversaries that it would respond to their acquisition of nuclear weapons by supplying equivalent capability to its allies. Before 1971, the possibility that the Soviet Union would provide a nuclear capability to Egypt was frequently suggested as a deterrent to an overt Israeli nuclear weapons program. Similarly, if the ally were officially informed of the threat (which may be a bad idea since if the threat fails to work, the pledge would then have to be honored), the likelihood of its going ahead on its own would decline. But employing a threat to promote proliferation in order actually to inhibit it is a risky strategy and should be followed only in very special circumstances.

Such a promise in a weaker form would avoid this latter problem to a large degree and still retain most of its original advantages. A superpower could inform or hint to its ally's adversary that nuclear weapons under its own control would be stationed on the ally's territory and would be available for its defense if the adversary acquired nuclear arms. This strategy requires not only an appropriate alliance relationship but also an ally that does not already have nuclear weapons stationed on its territory. The Soviet Union or China might use its relationship with North Korea in this way to damp possible South Korean nuclear ambitions.

Probably the most important and useful way to increase the security disincentives for proliferation is through the alliance systems of the Soviet Union and particularly the United States. Each superpower could suggest subtly, informally, but firmly that the continuance and strength of its security guarantees and other benefits to allies and clients depended on their refraining from going nuclear. The United States has used this type of persuasion with South Korea and Pakistan and may less openly be doing the same with Israel. The Soviet Union's influence over its Eastern European clients is more direct and quite powerful. Its preference to remain the only nuclear power within the Warsaw Pact will probably be decisive, even if never articulated. There is no evidence that the Soviet Union tried to use its influence on India.

Using alliance systems to increase security disincentives raises several important difficulties. Neither superpower will want to risk the alienation of an important ally by exerting strong pressure against nuclearization. This is perhaps the situation that the Soviet Union faced with India. Another problem is the limited reach of the alliance systems.

Many states that can be significantly pressured are precisely those whose existing alliance relationships make them least likely to go nuclear. In contrast, very little leverage exists against Argentina, Brazil, or Indonesia. Virtually none could be mounted against South Africa. Nonetheless, many potential proliferators are allies of the United States. Pressure within the alliance might be the most effective way to increase security disincentives for Taiwan, South Korea, Pakistan, Japan, Australia, and Iran. As already mentioned, American allies' uncertainty about adverse congressional reaction—even without direct pressure from the executive branch—will to some extent exert such pressure. Even here there are dangers, however. A threat to weaken security guarantees could encourage an ally's fears that its security was not of paramount interest to its patron and could thereby erode the credibility of those guarantees. The result could be precisely that which the threat was intended to prevent: the initiation of a nuclear weapons program.

Political disincentives should be sought as well. Particularly important are strengthening the international norm against proliferation and avoiding a sense of inevitability about it. Every additional party to the NPT strengthens the case of antinuclear advocates in domestic debates, but accession by near-nuclear states helps most. Ratification in 1975 by many Western European states and in 1976 by Japan was particularly significant. But for now the NPT system has probably gone about as far as can reasonably be expected. Japan may well be the last major state to ratify for some time. Egypt and Israel are not likely to do so as long as Middle East problems remain unsettled. Other important non-nuclear states will probably refrain for reasons of prestige or to maintain options. Still, the NPT is extremely useful in establishing an international norm despite these limitations. While every effort should be made to discourage renunciations that would undermine the whole system, primary attention should now turn to finding other means to increase the strength of the nonproliferation norm.

Any act or declaration by individual governments, groups of states, or international or regional organizations suggesting that acquisition of nuclear weapons is unacceptable would help. Nuclear-free zones and Security Council resolutions of the sort already discussed would not only reduce security and political incentives but also strengthen the international behavioral norm. Support by nuclear states of the NPT system and the IAEA safeguard program, including adequate financial and technical assistance, would be instrumental. Submission of their own civilian nuclear facilities to inspection would demonstrate their belief that the associated interference with sovereign prerogatives and commercial benefit is not onerous and, in any case, is necessary. Full participation in the NPT by France, China, and India would be particularly beneficial. As will be examined in detail below, international trade in nuclear technology and other facilities offers still further opportunities.

Another frequently proposed way to deter proliferation is through political and economic sanctions. Yet the recent historical evidence suggests that the international community's ability to impose and maintain meaningful sanctions is very limited. Unlike security guarantees, where one or a small number of states are critical, economic sanctions normally require wider cooperation to be effective. Beyond this practical problem, however, there is a more serious normative issue. The explosion of a nuclear device or any other act that heralds membership in the nuclear club is irreversible. Neither the knowledge and experience gained nor the act's psychological impact can be erased. It can only be punished or turned into an example for others. Seriously hurting the welfare of an entire population and perhaps the economic stability of a region to punish irreversible acts for which, in most cases, only governing elites are responsible seems a high price for very uncertain benefits. The world must live with a state after it has joined the nuclear club no less than before. For those who need the lesson, Versailles suffices to show that when states are punished too hard, they can sometimes visit the suffering on their afflicters.

Nonetheless, imposing relatively minor sanctions that have high political, psychological, and emotive content would have important symbolic value in preventing nuclear proponents in other countries from believing that going nuclear is costless. This would not, however, damage long-term relationships. Sanctions should come quickly and be accompanied by considerable verbal reprobation so that no government may perceive indecisiveness and indifference. Actions by non-nuclear states would be as important as—and in some instances more important than—those by nuclear states. Appropriate sanctions might include canceling expected visits of high government officials or activities conducted under scientific or cultural exchange programs, calling home an ambassador for consultations, terminating technical aid in the nuclear area (through the IAEA and by states directly), terminating other technical assistance and equipment sales that might contribute to the development of usable nuclear weapons systems, and at the extreme, perhaps even imposing some unfavorable terms of trade. Obviously a case-by-case review would be necessary, but interrupting food supplies or the sale of critical minerals—including enriched uranium for commercial reactors—would not be appropriate. The flow of funds, equipment, other resources needed for economic development, or conventional weapons could be temporarily halted pending review or slowed down to signal displeasure, but the threat of discontinuance should not be made a matter of declaratory policy lest it be tested and found wanting. Much more useful than a declaratory policy relying on sanctions after the fact would be moral suasion exerted beforehand and given force by subtle, implicit threats.

There is little more that can be said about the possibility of influencing domestic debates without referring to specific cases. There are many ways to strengthen antinuclear factions and undermine the arguments of their opponents. They include providing superpower security guarantees, exerting moral suasion, pursuing arms control, redistributing wealth and power, and especially strengthening the international norm against proliferation and avoiding the sense that the spread of weapons is inevitable. The general psychological environment will be critical. Direct intervention in domestic politics is also possible. Governments could intervene, individually or in concert, in decision making on nuclear issues or take other action that would strengthen the political position of an appropriate faction. But this could become a difficult and risky game to play during divisive domestic debate, whether public or private. Moreover, nonproliferation policy will not be the primary factor influencing the decision of what factions to support and by what means. In this situation as in others, states must protect themselves from being blackmailed and must beware of actions that could damage important long-term relationships in the name of nonproliferation.

FIVE

The Management of the International Nuclear Industry

The civilian nuclear power industry is an important potential source of weapons materials and provides relevant training and experience for technical personnel. The development of a nuclear power industry therefore would necessarily reduce the time required for a country to build a nuclear explosive once it decided to do so. The extent to which the time between making the decision and achieving the result (i.e., the *lead time*) would be reduced depends on how much of the fuel cycle was deployed domestically—in particular on whether a uranium enrichment facility or, more important, a fuel reprocessing plant was available. This relationship between a nuclear power industry and weapons proliferation has been universally recognized since the beginning of the nuclear age. It has led to an unprecedented degree of government control of the industry, particularly of trade in equipment, materials, and technology.

Nonetheless, this relationship has become the subject of renewed attention in recent years. With confidence in the security of oil supplies eroded by the Arab boycott of 1973 and the relative economics of competing energy resources altered by OPEC's cartel actions, more and more governments have become committed to or interested in building their own nuclear industries. India's nuclear test provided a dramatic reminder that a peaceful nuclear program can indeed provide materials for explosives. As a result, states, international organizations, non-governmental organizations, and individuals have been reevaluating their views of how the nuclear industry and particularly the diffusion of nuclear technology should be managed to minimize the risk of proliferation.[11] A widespread consensus has emerged within nuclear supplier states that tighter controls are necessary. But there is wide disagreement about how to achieve them. While the views are really quite diverse, a rough aggregation into three general approaches with quite different philosophical bases offers a useful analytical approximation.

The philosophy of the first approach may be called *technological denial*. It would preclude transfers of facilities that require weapons-grade materials for their operation or either produce or are capable of producing them. Technology, equipment, and facilities related to the sensitive parts of the fuel cycle—namely, spent-fuel reprocessing that produces plutonium usable for weapons, mixed-oxide fuel fabrication that uses plutonium to make reactor fuel, and uranium isotope enrichment that could be used to produce weapons-grade uranium—would not be transferred. If or when high-temperature gas-cooled or liquid metal fast breeder reactors that employ weapons-grade materials for fuel become commercially available, their transfer, too, would be proscribed. Other nuclear facilities including uranium oxide fuel fabrication technology, equipment, or facilities and currently available light- and heavy-water reactors could be exported to any state willing both to accept international safeguards and to promise formally not to divert materials for weapons purposes. The assumption underlying the technological denial approach is that severe constraints on the transfer of nuclear technology and facilities useful for acquiring weapons materials would maintain high economic, technological, and lead-time barriers against proliferation.

There are several stronger variations of the technological denial approach. One would permit transfer only to states that either have ratified the NPT or would accept safeguards on all nuclear facilities, including those in existence prior to the sale. The second would require the return of all plutonium-bearing irradiated fuel to the supplier state. Proponents of technological denial sometimes stress the importance of the leverage stemming from states' continuing dependence on their suppliers of enriched uranium and reprocessing services. They have in mind the suppliers' ability to make safeguards of material and facilities a

---

[11]One example is Ted Greenwood, George W. Rathjens, and Jack Ruina, *Nuclear Power Technology and Nuclear Weapons Proliferation*, Adelphi Paper no. 131, International Institute for Strategic Studies, London, 1976. Technical judgments used in the present paper are derived from this source.

condition of continuing supply as well as the implicit threat that services will be terminated if the customer state is perceived to violate agreements and move toward a nuclear explosives program. Technological denial is also sometimes linked to proposals for cartelization of the reactor export market, as a way to reduce commercial incentives to sell sensitive facilities.[12]

The philosophy of the second approach is perhaps best described as *dissuasion*. Its advocates argue that providing non-nuclear states with alternatives to indigenous reprocessing and enrichment technology will dissuade them from building their own. The underlying assumption is that these alternatives can satisfy all important reasons (other than those directly related to weapons manufacture) states may have to acquire these facilities themselves.

Finally, the third approach to managing the international nuclear industry may be characterized by the term *regulated transfer*. The transfer of any nuclear technology would be permitted, but only when accompanied by international safeguards and a bilateral agreement in which the purchasing state pledged not to use the technology, materials, or equipment as means for acquiring nuclear material for weapons purposes or to transfer technology, materials, or equipment to third parties without requiring equivalent assurances. The underlying assumptions are that (1) the combination of political assurances and safeguards will in fact prevent diversion from the civilian industry and (2) states that want to acquire weapons materials could do so on their own if other states denied assistance. Stronger versions that would permit transfer only to NPT parties or to states that accept safeguards on all existing nuclear facilities are also possible.

In evaluating these three approaches, several important factors must be taken into account. First, while only a limited number of states will need or can use large nuclear power plants in the 1980s, those that do undertake the very large investment required to establish a commercial industry will be motivated primarily by their concerns for energy supply. (Weapons options and the possible political benefits of improving technical capability can be achieved much more cheaply by acquiring small, inexpensive research facilities.) Having turned to nuclear power because it appears an economically attractive and enduring source of

---

[12]See for example Abraham A. Ribicoff, "A Market-Sharing Approach to the Nuclear Sales Problem," *Foreign Affairs*, vol. 54, no. 4 (July 1976), pp. 763–787.

reliable electrical energy, they will want to be sure that fuel-cycle services needed to operate their reactors efficiently, economically, and with minimum environmental cost will be available. The extent to which such states will feel satisfied relying on others for these services will depend primarily on how trustworthy they think potential suppliers are and how much matters of national sovereignty and prestige influenced their choices. For instance, states whose national pride and ambitions require a demonstrated ability to build strategically important industries are likely to want their own auxiliary fuel-cycle facilities.

Since the cost of the fuel cycle is a small part of any reactor program, economic issues will frequently be less important than a desire for independence. Some inefficiency will normally be acceptable if assuring a secure supply or enhancing national prestige requires it. Thus states may not care that the auxiliary facilities built to serve their small nuclear industries will be far below the minimum efficient size. If they do, they may build larger facilities and enter the international market. Some states might even see a commercial opportunity. In any event, small pilot plants would normally precede large commercial-scale facilities. Many, but certainly not all, states will simply insist on having their own fully integrated domestic fuel cycle.

Second, some states will insist that their spent fuel be reprocessed whether or not in their own facilities. Totally aside from the possible use of recovered plutonium for weapons, there are a number of motivations for states to acquire reprocessing technology.[13] One reason is to retrieve uranium and plutonium for recycle in current reactors. Given the anticipated costs of various components of the fuel cycle over the next 10 or so years, recycling now seems to involve a net cost rather than the previously anticipated net benefit. For heavy-water reactors, the economics are so unfavorable that the alternative, long-term storage of spent fuel, is preferable now and will remain so for many years. For the more common light-water reactor there are very great uncertainties in making a comparison. Nonetheless, the cost of reprocessing and recycle seems roughly commensurate with that of storage. The lack of a decisive

[13]See Greenwood et al., *Nuclear Power Technology*, and Ted Greenwood, "Why Reprocess?" in Abram Chayes and W. Bennett Lewis (eds.), *International Arrangements for Nuclear Fuel Cycle Facilities*, Ballinger Publications Co., Cambridge, Mass., 1977.

short-term economic argument for or against reprocessing in the light-water-reactor fuel cycle means that other considerations probably will dominate the choice.

One important consideration, particularly for nations lacking their own uranium supply and enrichment facilities, is the opportunity to reduce uranium imports by recycling fissile material from spent fuel. While recycling reduces by only 20 to 30 percent the requirements for uranium and enrichment, that amount might be considered quite significant by some governments. In addition, the uncertainty of future uranium supply and price might cause governments initiating nuclear industries to see recycling not only as a means of reducing imports but, more important, as a means of assuring fuel supply. Moreover, if the price of uranium rises steeply, the economics of reprocessing could become unambiguously advantageous.

The attractiveness of plutonium breeder reactors is closely related to the uncertainties of the uranium market. By converting the unfissile ^{238}U isotope that constitutes 99 percent of natural uranium into fissile plutonium faster than it consumes fuel, the plutonium breeder largely solves the fuel availability problem. While the commercial future of the breeders is currently very uncertain, there may be countries other than the current developers that will want to introduce them at an early date. To prepare for that possibility, they may want to reprocess light-water-reactor fuel to gain experience in dealing with plutonium in nuclear fuels and to accumulate the plutonium stockpile needed to start a breeder.

Several additional factors have particular relevance for the short run. If spent fuel is to be reprocessed eventually, there are economic reasons to do so early and thus avoid interim storage costs. In addition, some countries will want to deal with the nuclear waste management problem by first separating high-level wastes through reprocessing rather than storing spent fuel for a long time. A decision to reprocess fuel does not necessarily lead to construction of a domestic facility, but as already explained, it will sometimes do so. In such cases, government planners will probably be impressed with the length of time needed to build and learn to operate a commercial reprocessing facility and may well conclude that they should proceed immediately. Additionally of course, a government (or at least important components of its bureaucracy) may also want reprocessing technology in order to open weapons options.

Third, a refusal by current supplier states to transfer reprocessing and enrichment technology does not guarantee that potential recipients will have no access to weapons materials. A state could, totally on its own, build a small, low-pressure, graphite- or heavy-water-moderated, natural uranium reactor and a small reprocessing plant in order to obtain plutonium.[14] Even a commercial reprocessing plant is not unattainable for states with a fairly sophisticated chemical industry. The technology is straightforward and totally in the public domain. The major value of an outside supplier of reprocessing facilities is its engineering practice and know-how, not its knowledge of basic technology. Denying the transfer of reprocessing technology and equipment therefore is not equivalent to denying access to plutonium.

Enrichment technology, too, may become fairly readily available in the 1980s. The critical technology for the barriers used in gaseous-diffusion plants is still secret. Although all the nuclear weapons states except India have built such facilities, the undertaking would be a very difficult and costly route for countries wanting nuclear materials. Advanced centrifuge enrichment technology is also tightly held. Once the general techniques became more widely known, however, any state with a fairly advanced industrial capacity could build straightforward (although perhaps inefficient) centrifuges that would enable it to obtain highly enriched uranium. The same applies to the hydrodynamic nozzle technology developed in Germany. This is not even classified, and the required equipment may be easier to build and maintain than a centrifuge plant. South Africa seems to have developed a similar hydrodynamic technology, essentially on its own.

An enrichment facility built with any of these three technologies and designed to produce low-enrichment reactor fuel would be far from ideal for producing weapons-grade materials. Nonetheless, any state willing to pay the high economic price and prepared to forego some yield in reactor fuel while producing highly enriched uranium could use it that way. The great uncertainty in the enrichment area involves the laser isotope-separation techniques now being developed. If any of these techniques proves technically and commercially viable, which is very uncertain today, it might also be sufficiently simple and cheap to permit

[14]On the question of states building their own reprocessing facilities, see Greenwood et al., *Nuclear Power Technology and Nuclear Weapons Proliferation*, op. cit.

rather easy duplication and efficient enough to make high-enrichment, weapons-grade uranium readily available. The object here is not to assess in detail the status of uranium enrichment technology,[15] but simply to point out that while the plutonium production reactor and the reprocessing plant that can be built without outside help are probably the most attractive way to obtain weapons materials in the near future, viable uranium alternatives may also be close at hand.

Finally, the competitiveness of the international nuclear reactor market must be taken into account in evaluating the possible approaches to controlling nuclear exports.[16] Unlike a decade or so ago, when American firms controlled this market, today reactors can be bought from France, West Germany, Sweden, Switzerland, the Soviet Union, and Canada. India, the United Kingdom, Italy, and Japan have their own industries but are not marketing internationally. However, at least Japan might be expected to do so soon. The European vendors all believe they require export sales in order to achieve economies of scale for their domestic markets. They also seem to think that building nuclear bridges to important Third World countries will result in other trade and various political benefits. Canada, though, seems motivated more by a desire to assure the legitimacy and acceptance of its unique reactor design in the domestic market by selling to other countries.

The competition to sell reactors—particularly the light-water variety—is keen. Each government offers essentially the same product, and the costs, while difficult to determine, seem similar. The competition is frequently manifested in other areas, therefore. These could include financing arrangements, assurances of enriched uranium supplies, the supply of additional fuel-cycle facilities, or a willingness to compromise on safeguards and other antiproliferation requirements. A negotiated agreement among the seven primary or potential supplier states (Canada, France, Japan, the Soviet Union, the United Kingdom, the United States, and West Germany) has now guaranteed—so long as it remains in effect—that competition will not include compromising on safeguards and physical security requirements. Rivalry in the other areas can be expected to continue. West Germany, for instance, won the

[15]For such an assessment, see ibid.
[16]See Paul C. Joskow, "The International Nuclear Industry Today," *Foreign Affairs,* vol. 54, no. 4 (July 1976), pp. 788–803.

contest to sell reactors to Brazil largely because it was willing to supply a fully integrated fuel cycle.[17]

Efforts made by the United States, during a series of London meetings, to encourage other suppliers to subscribe to its policy of refusing to sell reprocessing and enrichment facilities have failed so far. The French and the West Germans fear that their ability to compete with American reactor vendors would decrease unless they could sweeten their own offers with package deals. They may want to build pilot plants for untested technology with financing provided by other states. Moreover, they seem to have a different view of the preferred mechanisms to discourage proliferation than do most Americans. Without French and German cooperation, the United States has relatively little leverage. France's reprocessing technology is more advanced than that of the United States. And Germany is willing to sell its hydrodynamic enrichment technology. Moreover, the United States is far behind the Europeans in breeder reactor technology, the transfer of which would raise precisely the same issues as the transfer of reprocessing technology.

What action should be taken, then, by supplier states acting individually or together to achieve regulation and control? To the extent that security of fuel supply and concern with nuclear waste management contribute to the desire to acquire enrichment or reprocessing facilities, supplier states and the international community can act through the market to reduce these incentives. Attractive alternatives to reprocessing, the use of plutonium, and the construction of indigenous enrichment and reprocessing facilities can and should be provided to non-nuclear states.

One alternative to enrichment is the CANDU natural uranium reactor. Indeed, since it utilizes uranium more efficiently than do light-water reactors, its widespread use would also delay the time when a plutonium economy would become economically attractive. Given the large quantities of plutonium produced in any commercial reactor, the fact that a CANDU produces slightly more plutonium than a light-water reactor per unit of electric power generated is unimportant. Moreover, it is compensated for by the lower concentration of plutonium per unit of spent fuel that results from the rapid consumption of natural uranium

[17]William Lowrance, "Nuclear Futures for Sale: West Germany to Brazil 1975," *International Security,* vol. 2, October 1976.

fuel. The quality of the plutonium produced is not better for weapons than that obtainable from a light-water reactor. However, given the strong commitment of all nuclear supplier countries except Canada to light-water reactors, widespread reliance on CANDU-type reactors seems very unlikely to develop.

Extensive and assured supplies of relatively cheap uranium or reliance on a thorium conversion or breeding cycle would be alternatives to reprocessing for the purpose of recycling fissile plutonium. The possibility of relying on thorium is discussed elsewhere in this volume. Efforts are now under way in the United States and Canada to inventory uranium resources. This activity should be extended to as many other areas of the world as possible. In addition, attempts should be made to expand uranium mining and milling capacity. The less the likelihood of uranium shortages in the next 10 to 20 years and the greater the diversity of suppliers, the less likely states will be to reprocess and recycle or to plan on early introduction of breeders. Efforts to guarantee long-term supplies of uranium would be assisted if Australia were willing to create significant production capacity and major suppliers would avoid cartelization of the market.

The need for a secure supply of enrichment services is as absolute for any operator of a light-water reactor as the supply of uranium itself. Security concerns will therefore dominate a government's decision on whether or not to rely on others for these services. While the likelihood of a shortage of uranium separation capacity over the next 10 to 15 years seems significantly less now than it did before the recent spate of cancellations and extensions of reactor building programs, avoiding future expectations of shortage should have high priority. This requires planning and timely construction of facilities to increase capacity beyond the current projections. Market uncertainties and the threat that new technology will rapidly render any new facility obsolescent may discourage private investment in the United States. If they do, the United States government should be prepared either to expand its own capacity or to provide sufficient price support guarantees to private interests. But other nuclear weapons states and current suppliers of enrichment services could, and should, also consider expansion. Sufficient diversity of suppliers is almost as important as adequate supply in minimizing the likelihood that the provision of services will be curtailed for political reasons.

States without their own uranium might be induced to rely on external enrichment suppliers if access to natural uranium were linked to extended contracts for enrichment services. They might perceive such an arrangement as offering greater security of supply than would relying on an indigenous enrichment plant in conjunction with imported natural uranium. Such a linkage would be difficult to create if it required extensive cooperation among major uranium suppliers and those currently having enrichment capacity. However, it will to some extent develop automatically if plans are fulfilled to build enrichment facilities in South Africa and Australia.

Stockpiling natural or, preferably, enriched uranium would also lower the danger of supply curtailment and thereby reduce the incentives for states to build their own enrichment plants and to reprocess spent fuel. The cost of carrying the inventory, though small in comparison with the overall cost of the fuel cycle, would still be substantial. Assuming that suppliers were indeed interested in encouraging stockpiling, long-term contracts for enrichment could be used to provide financial assistance. No significant stockpiling is feasible, however, unless uranium mining, milling, and enrichment capacities expand beyond that needed to supply immediate needs. The United States and other suppliers of enrichment services should act to assure sufficient capacity to permit stockpile accumulations by purchasing states.

In order to discourage states from reprocessing their spent fuel and recycling plutonium as a means of dealing with nuclear waste, nuclear supplier states could create spent-fuel repository sites and offer storage services to non-nuclear states. Such an arrangement could be made particularly attractive if the storage cost were paid for or subsidized by supplier states. In order to allow non-nuclear states to derive value from spent fuel without actually using the plutonium, suppliers could offer to purchase spent fuel or to trade equivalent quantities of low enriched uranium for it. For the latter arrangement to be feasible, sufficient quantities of natural uranium and sufficient enrichment capacity would have to be available.

Despite the creation of such mechanisms, some states will no doubt insist on obtaining and recycling plutonium. Rather than concentrating solely on efforts to dissuade or prevent states from doing so, therefore, prudent planning requires the creation of mechanisms that will keep the associated dangers as low as possible. It would be far better for non-nuclear states to obtain plutonium under controlled conditions from traditional nuclear supplier states than to induce the construction of indigenous reprocessing facilities in non-nuclear states by denying them access to reprocessing services. Non-nuclear states that insist on using plutonium should be encouraged to rely on others for reprocessing services. The creation of sufficient reprocessing capacity in several different countries would permit reliable access to services at competitive prices and would be the most important inducement. A standing offer by reprocessors to deal with wastes themselves would also help. Many states, after all, lack geological structures suitable for permanent storage of high-level nuclear wastes. For the forseeable future, the European reprocessing cartel, United Reprocessors, is the only guaranteed supplier of services, though its prices are unattractively high and its expansion plans are in doubt. The advantages of providing alternatives to indigenous reprocessing in non-nuclear states argue strongly for an early American decision to open the partially completed reprocessing plant in Barnwell, South Carolina, and to allocate as much of its capacity as can be absorbed to the international market. Environmentally acceptable waste management technologies should also be demonstrated on a priority basis.

From a nonproliferation standpoint, any reliance by non-nuclear states on plutonium fuel is less satisfactory than sole reliance on low-enriched or natural uranium. The latter would not be usable for weapons production; the former would be. Shipping plutonium only in mixed-oxide form or "spiking" it with a gamma ray emitter can make handling more difficult but would still not prevent states from fabricating explosives out of imported plutonium. The risks can be greatly reduced, however, if recovered plutonium were stored at the reprocessing site in the nuclear supplier state and shipped to non-nuclear user states only in small quantities as needed for actual reactor use and under IAEA safeguards. Plutonium stockpiles would thereby be avoided, and the costs of diversion would be raised.

Multinational (perhaps regional) or international fuel-cycle centers and spent-fuel repositories have been proposed as another way to induce states not to build their own sensitive facilities. These centers appear to have both the advantages of relying on nationally owned external suppliers and the problems involved in handling plutonium. Their major additional advantage is that by offering partial ownership and control to many states, these centers would to some extent satisfy security, political, and symbolic concerns that might otherwise induce governments to build national plants. Since these motivations may well influence some states, the IAEA's efforts to stimulate the initiation of multinational reprocessing centers deserve support. These and other international efforts will move slowly, however, and should not yet be considered a substitute for individual suppliers' offering alternatives to reprocessing and expanding their own reprocessing and enrichment capacity. These should be matters of immediate concern and action.

If a variety of these actions were taken, many states might lose interest in acquiring their own indigenous sensitive fuel-cycle facilities. Others might be willing to delay. For some, however, dissuasion by these market mechanisms will not succeed. They will still want their own facilities. They might be motivated by a sense of inevitability, by concerns about national sovereignty and prestige, by commercial considerations, by a residual anxiety about security of supply, or by the desire to create weapons options. This expectation that success will not be total is not sufficient reason to abandon the strategy of dissuasion. It should be vigorously pursued while at the same time being augmented by other action to deal with those states for which it will not succeed. The two alternatives are technological denial and regulated transfer.

Technological denial is not very attractive. In the absence of severe American pressure that might be very damaging to bilateral relationships and perhaps to the structure of the NATO alliance, France and West Germany are unlikely to refrain from selling enrichment and reprocessing facilities and technology and eventually breeder reactors and mixed-oxide-fuel fabrication facilities. The commercial and political benefits are perceived to be too high. In addition, if the French and Germans were not today offering to sell reprocessing or enrichment plants, the Argentinians, the Taiwanese, the Indians, or the South Africans might do so within the next decade. While delay is not without some benefit, agreement among the industrialized states alone simply would not eliminate an international market in sensitive fuel-cycle technology for very long.

More important, refusing to sell sensitive technology does not deny access to it. Any government capable of managing a commercial nuclear industry could build its own facilities to produce enough plutonium for a modest weapons program. Most of those for which market dissuasion will not succeed can now or would within a decade be able to build their own pilot-scale commercial reprocessing or enrichment plants. Some, particularly those such as Pakistan and Taiwan that are dependent on American security guarantees and alliance relationships, might be persuaded not to do so. However, such persuasion not only might carry a high political cost, but it might also weaken the credibility of the guarantees and accelerate the process it is meant to impede. States such as South Africa and Brazil are not particularly susceptible to such leverage.

There is another cost to be incurred by adopting a technological denial approach. An agreement among industrialized states to deny Third World countries technology with significant potential economic benefit and major symbolic value is likely to damage efforts to reach political accommodation between the world's rich and poor states. Such an agreement could be interpreted as violating obligations under the NPT. More important, it would be seen as an effort to interfere with sovereign prerogatives and to prevent Third World states from achieving industrial development, economic prosperity, and equality with and independence from the industrialized world. Any attempts by industrial states jointly to manage the reactor market as a means of reducing French and German commercial incentives to offer enrichment and reprocessing facilities would no doubt be interpreted similarly.

This cost might disappear if agreement could be reached differently. Currently the initiative lies with advanced industrialized states; the Third World does not participate, nor is there a role for international organizations beyond the IAEA's negotiation and implementation of safeguard agreements. A policy of technological denial that was agreed to in a forum with Third World participation—or, better, as the result of a Third World initiative—would be less likely to make the management of the nuclear industry into a divisive North-South issue. The difficulty is that such a process is unlikely. Many of the larger, wealthier, and influential Third World nations will find the incentives to acquire their own facilities too great to forswear the option of doing so. In addition, even Third World states that did not want their own facilities would probably not want actually to deny themselves industrial capacity and thereby imply that they were less trustworthy than industrialized states. That reaction, at least, has been the case with the NPT. While desirable, then, a North-South agreement or one initiated by Southern states seems extremely unlikely.

As a general approach for dealing with states that insist on acquiring sensitive nuclear technology, technological denial is costly and promises little benefit. It should be used only in particular high-risk cases. No transfers of sensitive technology should be made to states whose governments are suspected of a calculated ploy to gain help in a weapons program and a willingness to disregard political assurances against diversion or whose political systems are so unstable and uncertain that the emergence of a future government willing to renounce previous assurances is fairly high. Indeed, in the most blatant instances, not even power or research reactors should be supplied. If the state is indeed determined to acquire weapons, this denial will result only in delay. While moderately valuable in itself, it may be the best alternative available and provide time for the state's calculation of costs and benefits to change or be influenced.

Except in such high-risk cases, the regulated transfer approach offers the potential for greater effectiveness in inhibiting proliferation and involves less cost. Supplier states should be willing to sell sensitive facilities to those states that cannot be persuaded to rely on others to provide the desired services. Indeed, the eagerness of these states to purchase facilities rather than construct their own may be seen as an opportunity. The economic and technical barriers against access to fissile material, which will inevitably decline, can be replaced with institutional and political barriers, which will probably be more effective in the long run. The civilian nuclear power industry can thus be institutionally separated from the problem of nuclear weapons proliferation.

For states party to the NPT, acceptance of regulated transfers would strengthen and extend already existing obligations. For states not party to the NPT, it would provide substitute impediments that are almost equivalent: the primary differences would be that they were tied to the process of transfer and would not necessarily include a formal renunciation of the right to develop nuclear explosives. When possible, a commitment should be obtained to place all existing nuclear facilities under safeguard. If this proved to be strongly resisted, the decision to sell should be made on a case-by-case basis. Imposing restrictions on future facilities could still be beneficial if the risks of diversion did not seem too high and other political considerations did not suggest the contrary.

Regulated transfers would be appropriate even, or perhaps particularly, in instances in which a nuclear energy bureaucracy—with or without assistance from the military and other domestic allies—appears to be trying to push a nation inexorably toward a weapons program. If such governments could be encouraged to accept safeguards and enter into bilateral agreements constraining their future options, their weapons proponents would have greater difficulty. Indeed, since in such cases nuclear advocates could be expected to favor domestic development of enrichment and reprocessing technology rather than imports with strings attached, vigorous marketing may be necessary. Depending on the evolution of its own plans, Argentina might become a case in point.

Sensitive technology should be transferred only under certain conditions which should be applied also to nonsensitive materials, technology, and facilities. First, purchasers must agree to submit to international safeguards. This obligation should have unlimited duration and be without any means of unilateral termination. Safeguards must also apply to ''replication'' of the technology, which should be defined in as broad a manner as possible. Brazil and West Germany, for instance, agreed to consider any equipment and facilities constructed or operated within a 20-year period as unequivocally based on the transferred technology and thus subject to safeguards. Theirs is precisely the sort of commitment that is needed; the longer the duration of unequivocally broad applicability, the better. Second, purchasers must forswear for all time the right to use transferred material, equipment, or technology for a nuclear explosives program. Again, the ambiguous issue of when new facilities are no longer to be considered derived from transferred technology can be resolved by stipulating an arbitrary period of time. During the specified period, all new facilities would be considered derivative. When it ended, this commitment would still apply, but debate over interpretation would be possible. Third, transfers to other countries should be governed by the same conditions and—in order to prevent any transfers to particularly high-risk countries—should be subject to the initial supplier state's approval. These are precisely the requirements that have been endorsed by the nuclear supplier states in their London meetings and applied to recent transfers. They are to be welcomed as a significant achievement.

Of course, one may question the worth of paper commitments and IAEA safeguards when a state receiving technology and equipment could, if it chose to ignore or renounce them, have access to weapons materials. The IAEA safeguards in particular can be justly criticized as providing less than complete assurance that states are fulfilling their obligations. Moreover, the problems may well worsen. As the international industry grows and diversifies, the demands imposed on the IAEA's inspection capacities will be difficult to meet. Simply attracting adequate personnel, designing an appropriate information system, and managing the transition from preeminent nuclear promotion responsibilities to an equal or overriding concern with a safeguard function will be very challenging tasks for the agency. Handling the political issues of when and how to question possible violations will be even more difficult. But even if it is not technically foolproof, the IAEA safeguards program is extremely useful. It probably provides sufficient risk of detection to make attempts at diversion very unlikely. Its existence assists negotiations of political assurances between states by providing an international and nominally objective substitute for what would otherwise have to be a series of bilateral inspection programs. Perhaps more important, it embodies in institutional form the international norm of nonproliferation. Its intervention into nuclear programs fosters organizational procedures and institutional commitments that deepen and reinforce the physical and psychological separation of civilian nuclear programs from any possible military application. These are precisely the sort of institution-building mechanisms that are most important. The efforts of the IAEA deserve the support of all nations; they should be improved where possible and guarded against erosion of confidence and effectiveness.

Sovereign states can violate commitments or deny IAEA safeguard personal access to facilities. New governments can attain power and not feel bound by obligations undertaken by predecessors. Where such risks seem high, technological denial is the appropriate response. But if incorrect judgments are made, the only recourse is to apply sanctions after the fact. While reliance on safeguards and political commitments is therefore less than perfect, in many states it is the best means available for separating civilian nuclear programs from possible weapons programs. Except for NPT parties, states that built their own facilities because they had been denied assistance would be under no obligation to accept safeguards and would have given no assurances not to use them for weapons purposes. An opportunity to impose constraints would have been lost.

Moreover, the political commitments of governments are far from meaningless. They are solemn political undertakings, entered into only after internal debates and consensus-building processes are completed. They establish a norm for behavior and planning for the obligated state as well as its neighbors and adversaries. They commit the prestige and credibility of the purchasing government and, at least as important, of a supplier that will not take lightly a violation of commitments made to it. While the time period during which all new technology must be considered derivative may be limited, the basic commitment not to use transferred technology for military purposes will apply indefinitely. Moreover, the duration of unequivocal interpretations should be long enough to establish firmly the norm of behavior within the government bureaucracy and make later departure very difficult. Any continuing cooperation and transfer of new technology would, in addition, have the effect of extending this period of unambiguity.

In short, regulated transfer provides admittedly less than absolute certainty that states receiving sensitive technology will not eventually use it for weapons. But such certainty is not possible in any event. The approach does, however, provide much greater leverage than would outright refusals to transfer sensitive facilities to insistent states. The assumption that economic and technical barriers can be maintained over the long run is invalid and would provide no comparable political commitments. Transfer of technology which fosters safeguards and strong political commitments is thus a desirable extension of or substitute for the NPT. Because it involves bilateral as well as international commitments, it may in some cases be even more effective. Employed along with actions intended to dissuade states from building their own sensitive facilities (and with the possible exception of some particularly high-risk cases), it seems the best way to manage the international nuclear industry.

SIX

Non-State Entities

Non-state entities acting independently, be they individuals or large, organized revolutionary organizations, and whatever their motivations, lack the legitimacy (both in the possession and use of force and in the control of territory) that international law and tradition afford to sovereign states. Thus they form a special category in the analysis of nonproliferation. Nuclear tests by a country on territory it controls, whatever the political implications, are not considered acts of belligerency. However, a detonation by a non-state entity anywhere except on the high seas would necessarily be on territory claimed by a sovereign state and would necessarily elicit severe retaliation and reprisals.

Just as states employ force or the threat of force for political purposes, so do organized groups of revolutionaries, guerrillas, and terrorists. Thus they can be distinguished, at least for analytical purposes, from criminals motivated by profit and from psychopaths who derive psychic gratification from violence. In fact, however, this distinction is not clear-cut. Small terrorist groups, such as the Japanese Red Army, the Symbionese Liberation Army, and the Baader-Meinhof Gang, act largely out of frustration and alienation. While being motivated by a diffuse political ideology, but lacking nationalistic orientation, they may actually have more in common with criminals and psychopaths than with large, nationally oriented groups such as the Palestinian Liberation Organization, the Irish Republican Army, the Tupamaros, or the Eritrean Liberation Front. All of these groups and individuals are of concern in thinking about non-state use of nuclear weapons. However, since the problems relevant to criminals, psychopaths, and small terrorist groups are quite different from those raised by large revolutionary organizations, they will be considered separately.

There is no need here to open the controversial issue of how various non-state entities might go about fabricating a nuclear explosive or precisely how difficult it would be to do so. Our concern here is more with motivation than with feasibility. Suffice it to say that obtaining weapons-grade material and fabricating even a crude nuclear explosive are reasonably difficult. They require substantial financial and technical resources, a capability for planning and coordinating complex activities, and sufficient cohesiveness and motivation to assure continuity of effort over an extended period of time. Assuming equal incentive, a sizable, organized group is much more likely to succeed than an individual or any small group except in the unlikely event that its members have extensive training in relevant technical areas.

Revolutionaries strive actively to destroy or topple an established political authority or to seek major political or territorial concessions. In doing so they might consider using nuclear weapons in conjunction with guerrilla, terrorist, or traditional military tactics.[18] Nuclear explosions might be used to disable or impede the operation of the government's deployed forces or to destroy important economic values or symbolic targets. They could also be used to intimidate; to attract attention to a cause; to undermine the legitimacy and authority of a government; to deter the carrying out of targeted activities; or to induce terror, fear, or alarm. They seem particularly attractive for the latter purpose because of the sheer extent of their concentrated power and the strong taboo against their use. The psychological impact of a nuclear explosion would be enormous and global no matter how few actual casualties were caused. There is probably no more dramatic or horrifying weapon of terror or more effective means of instilling fear of the perpetrating organization than a nuclear explosion. It would guarantee immediate, extensive, and continuing world attention.

Yet the power, destructiveness, and radioactive nature of nuclear explosives are potential disadvantages as well. An explosion in a populated area would result in large-scale and wanton killing. Even in their

---

[18]They might also consider seizing or damaging nuclear facilities or stealing nuclear material for reasons other than to manufacture weapons. While of great concern, such activities are not considered here.

terrorist activities, revolutionary groups do not see killing as useful in and of itself. While people are frequently killed during terrorist attacks, the killing is usually limited, controlled, and calculated to serve one or more specific purposes. Mass killing would have no additional function beyond those served by conventional explosives. The immediate aims of terrorist acts (as opposed to the ultimate objectives of terrorists) have been quite limited. Grand objectives simply cannot be achieved within the time scale of a single act of terror and may simply be unattainable. Governments will not destroy themselves or radically alter the societies they govern in direct response to threat or coercion, no matter how serious. To date, revolutionary terrorists have refrained from many very destructive acts they could accomplish without nuclear weapons. Presumably there has been no particular need or reason to do them.

Despite their revolutionary program and ideology, nationally oriented revolutionary groups have their own extensive stakes in the status quo which they would be loath to jeopardize by resorting to nuclear explosives. For instance, they seek international respectability as a means to legitimize their requests for political support and other aid. Groups engaged in protracted struggle include this endeavor as part of their revolutionary activities. Others may have time to establish respectability only after gaining power. In either case, any use of nuclear weapons that caused widespread destruction would seriously undermine claims to respectability and thus discourage states from granting recognition and support.

More important, any revolutionary group needs a base of support for sanctuary, supplies, and weapons. For groups operating within the territory controlled or claimed by the target government and relying on the support of the general population, a use of nuclear weapons that killed large numbers of people or destroyed important national values or symbols would risk alienating that support and inducing severe repression. The target government would surely gain significant popular support and possibly external aid for its efforts to suppress the perpetrating organization or retaliate against its supporters. Extreme tactics of torture and the unbridled use of military power would be condoned and assisted by the population as never before. Indeed, the likelihood of a popularly based revolutionary group surviving long after its first destructive use of nuclear weapons within the state it was seeking to control seems small. Even revolutionaries that do not rely on popular support (such as military dissidents) are not likely to use nuclear weapons against significant military or symbolic targets. No individual or group wants to achieve control of a nation in which the population and politically significant elites are so alienated that it is unable to govern.

Revolutionary or terrorist groups that receive sanctuary, protection, or significant resources from governments other than the one under attack would risk losing that support as well if they used nuclear weapons. All states have an interest in maintaining a taboo against non-state possession of nuclear weapons and in punishing and suppressing its violators. Sanctuary states in particular would view a nuclear revolutionary group within their borders as a threat to their own security. They would be similarly reluctant to assist the rise to power in a neighboring state of a group whose nuclear capability would make it that much more difficult to control or restrain. As the collapse of the Kurdish rebellion following Iran's withdrawal of support, the rapid decline in airline hijacking after the U.S.–Cuban extradition agreement in 1973, and the history of piracy have demonstrated, the loss of sanctuary and foreign support is fatal to terrorist or revolutionary organizations.

The one way that a revolutionary group might be able to use a nuclear explosive destructively to further its cause, yet not elicit overwhelming opposition from those it was seeking to govern, would be to direct it against an external power, perhaps the United States or Soviet Union, that was supporting the opposed government. The purpose would be to persuade the external power to cease its support. A crude weapon delivered in a boat to a harbor or coastal area would serve the purpose. Although such an operation might be conducted covertly, the revolutionary group could not expect to derive any coercive value from its action if it remained anonymous. Significant costs would therefore be incurred. First, the group's claim to international legitimacy would be jeopardized. Second, its own protectors might reduce or remove their support because of their reluctance to assist a group having nuclear weapons to become a sovereign entity. Third, the target state, particularly if it possessed a large military establishment, would probably redouble its efforts—whether or not supported by states in the geographical region in which the group operated—to eradicate the perpetrating organization. Nuclear use against either the Soviet Union or the United States could be expected to result in immediate and ruthless retaliation.

There are nondestructive ways in which a revolutionary group could use a nuclear weapon. These include detonations deep underground, deep in the ocean, in a remote and unpopulated area, and at high altitudes. Deep underground implacement is very difficult if even reasonable confidence is required that extensive venting will not occur. A deep ocean explosion would not vent but, like one deep underground, might not become publicized in the unlikely event that governments with appropriate detection equipment chose to suppress their intelligence information and succeeded in doing so. A remote land area that was accessible and was governed by a sovereignty that the revolutionary group was willing to affront could provide a relatively costless opportunity to demonstrate nuclear capability. Still, the explosion's long-range, long-term, unpredictable, and uncontrollable radiological effects could be expected to act as an enduring goad for revenge against the perpetrators. Perhaps the best way that a revolutionary group could demonstrate its nuclear capacity would be a high-altitude explosion. If sufficiently high, it would cause minimal fallout and no damage beyond retinal burns to those who looked directly at the fireball. With a careful choice of location, it could be very dramatic. There is ample evidence to suggest that obtaining an appropriate airplane would not be very difficult.

A revolutionary group that employed nuclear explosives in any of these nondestructive ways might avoid loss of legitimacy, loss of support, and severe retaliation; at least it might suffer them to a lesser degree. While nondestructive use might be linked to short-term objectives such as inducing terror or gaining publicity, it would be more fruitful as a component of a long-term political strategy. A revolutionary group with demonstrated nuclear capability could exploit nuclear threats against military or urban-industrial targets for coercive purposes. It might thereby be able to achieve political objectives short of overthrow of the opposed government or to exert significant influence on political events. Nondestructive use therefore seems to be the most serious threat from revolutionary groups in possession of nuclear weapons.

Nuclear incentives might be stronger and disincentives weaker for smaller, less capable terrorist organizations that are neither nationally oriented nor in any sense embodiments of the political aspirations of a religious, cultural, or linguistic group. Since they are neither motivated by a well-articulated political program nor tied to a geographical area, these groups (such as the Japanese Red Army or the Baader-Meinhof

Gang) have much to gain and little to lose from publicity and the creation of panic. Almost all governments already are actively seeking their destruction. With less stake in the status quo than revolutionary groups with national aims, they might be more likely to use nuclear weapons destructively. Like either individual criminals or psychopaths or small groups of them, however, small terrorist groups generally would not have the resources or support—as nationally oriented revolutionary movements more often would—necessary either to obtain weapons material or, having accomplished that task, to fabricate an explosive. More important, the historical record suggests that even small groups of political extremists, criminals, and psychopaths do not generally perceive mass murder and widespread devastation as useful. Even though non-nuclear means to these ends have long existed, their use has rarely been contemplated seriously.

This discussion suggests that non-state entities are likely to use a nuclear weapon in inverse proportion to their ability to obtain one and that those most able to acquire nuclear weapons would probably use them, if at all, in a manner calculated to minimize destruction. When this analysis is considered with the foregoing observations about the degree of difficulty of making nuclear explosives and the extent of the incentives and disincentives to use them, it leads to the conclusion that the likelihood of nuclear destruction by non-state entities is quite small and that of any use only slightly greater. Nonetheless, this optimistic assessment does not mean that the likelihood is zero even for a very destructive explosion or that there is no cause for concern and appropriate caution. Indeed, while these conclusions seem to be reasonable extrapolations from the past, the future is as unpredictable in this respect as in any other.

There are several ways to keep the likelihood of nuclear use by non-state entities small or even to reduce it. Most important is to make stealing or otherwise obtaining a weapon or weapons material exceedingly difficult by adequately protecting all fissile material and particularly all weapons stockpiles. Guarding against large armed attacks would be very expensive, perhaps prohibitively so, but protection against the small groups and individuals that pose the greatest threat is less difficult. Nations in which there is a history of violent and socially disruptive struggles for power or in which terrorist groups have been able to operate with relative impunity pose the greatest risks. If they acquire civilian power facilities, stringent measures should be taken to reduce the chances that nuclear material can be seized under any conditions ranging from tranquility to extreme disintegration. Similar security measures will also be necessary if such states actually acquire nuclear weapons. Unfortunately, such requirements are easier to enunciate than to implement.

Governments could also try to anticipate which non-state groups are most likely to seek a nuclear capability and to suppress or dissuade them. For criminals, psychopaths, and small terrorist groups, suppression would be appropriate but has its limitations. Even an extensive intelligence capability may be unable to identify high-risk individuals or groups until they have acted. Some observers argue that the level of government surveillance or other sorts of intrusions into citizens' lives which would be necessary for potential nuclear terrorists to be recognized and suppressed would significantly undermine the foundations of democratic societies. Their claim is based upon assumptions and conclusions—about the ease of fabricating or stealing nuclear explosives and about the likelihood that someone will try to obtain weapons and will use them if successful—that are quite different from those reached in this analysis. There is indeed a limit to the degree of suppression possible and desirable in democratic societies and a limit to its effectiveness anywhere. However, these limits seem far beyond what is necessary to render the likelihood of nuclear terrorism very small. Indeed, the primary focus should be on protection of materials, not surveillance and suppression of potential terrorists.

The matter of identification and dissuasion is more complex for nationally oriented revolutionary groups. States are likely to support or oppose such groups for political reasons unconnected to nuclear potential. Changing a policy of opposition to one of support of a group because it seems about to launch a nuclear program would provide a major incentive for others to follow suit and would thereby expose states to easy manipulation and blackmail. It is not, therefore, either a useful or a likely method of dissuasion. Instead, states backing revolutionary groups would be well advised to make their support conditional on nuclear abstinence. While this position cannot be made formal by treaty or public statement, it nonetheless should and probably will be adopted and implemented subtly as a matter of pure self-interest.

Nuclear threats by non-state entities are a matter quite different from nuclear use. For nationally oriented revolutionary groups, the incentives and disincentives for employing nuclear threats would not be very different from those already discussed for nuclear use, although perhaps not as strong. The primary incentive would be the desire to coerce, extort, or terrorize. The primary disincentives would be the loss of legitimacy and support and the possibility of increased active repression.

But nuclear threats can be made by anyone (including criminals, psychopaths, and pranksters), for any purpose, with only a phone call or a letter. However, making the threat believable, whether to government officials or to the general public, is another matter. Under some circumstances, proof of possession of nuclear material or perhaps publication of a weapons design might be necessary. Yet even a totally unsupported threat that is well publicized might be all that is required to cause public alarm. The requirement would surely depend on the particular circumstances, including how the threat is made and how responsible officials and the media react. Although nuclear threats have been made in the United States and the Middle East and may very well be made again, none so far has been credible.

There seems to be little that can be done to prevent such threats except to minimize the expectation that they will result in benefit or personal gratification. For that purpose, the less discussion of threats the better, except when discussion focuses on states' determination to resist decisively. Since fashions seem to develop in the activities of criminals, psychopaths, and pranksters and since an important objective of terrorist threats, no less than of attacks, is publicity, governments at all levels should attempt to conceal the existence of a nuclear threat except, of course, if there is good reason to believe it is real. In this effort they should seek the understanding and cooperation of the media.

Reactions of resistance and minimal publicity may seem a lame prescription for deterring nuclear threats, but short of pervasive state surveillance of citizens' activities, there appear to be no alternatives. The reactions to and outcomes of the first few threats will strongly influence the frequency of subsequent ones. Protection and monitoring of fissile material is again critical; if sufficient confidence exists that no fissile material has been lost, nuclear threats will not be credible and cannot be real.

An international convention for the suppression of nuclear terrorism has been proposed, modeled after the Convention for the Suppression of

Unlawful Seizure of Aircraft of 1971. It would be useful to the extent that it fostered the adoption of stringent physical security measures by all states, assured the denial of sanctuary to nuclear terrorists, and established a useful norm of national behavior. But its usefulness for deterrence would be limited. Those groups or individuals most likely to engage in nuclear terror or threat either are actively pursued anyway by national and international security organizations or would operate solely within the national borders of a single state.

More important are the encouragement of national governments' efforts to develop and employ very strict physical protection measures and the strengthening of the IAEA's role in assisting them. Adequate physical protection standards, no less than adequate safeguards, should be and are increasingly becoming a prerequisite to the sale of nuclear reactors or fuel-cycle equipment and technology. The recent nuclear suppliers' agreement included a provision requiring states purchasing nuclear facilities and materials to furnish rather stringent physical protection. Industrialized states with already large nuclear programs should lead the way by sharing technology and experience and, where necessary, by offering subsidies. Finally, the likelihood of social and political disorder that might so erode normal physical protection arrangements as to make access to weapons-grade material relatively easy for non-state entities should be seriously considered in decisions about which countries pose too high a risk for the transfer of reactors and other fuel-cycle facilities.

SEVEN

A Strategy for Nonproliferation

The preceding analysis has suggested that the primary incentives for states to acquire nuclear weapons emerge from regional security considerations; the desire to enhance national power and prestige; and an eagerness to achieve regional hegemony, leadership among a group of states with common interests, or status as a global power. Some states might also want nuclear security against the global nuclear powers, the United States and Soviet Union. The primary disincentives are unwillingness to encourage other states to acquire nuclear weapons, reluctance to disturb stable political relationships, fear that once available weapons might be used, concern with maintaining control over arsenals in the face of civil disruption or terrorist attack, acceptance of the international behavioral norm proscribing their acquisition, and knowledge of the domestic economic or political costs of obtaining weapons material and carrying out a weapons development program.

Non-state entities will see nuclear use as appealing mainly because of the scale of destruction attainable through the weapons and the assurance of widespread publicity that would follow. They could also use or threaten to use nuclear weapons for purposes of blackmail or coercion. The primary disincentives are the difficulty of obtaining materials and fabricating weapons, the lack of ways to use nuclear weapons to be more effective than conventional means in achieving desired objectives, and the fear that nuclear terror would lead to loss of legitimacy and elicit strong suppressive action.

While these incentives might seem quite significant to some states and non-state entities, they would appear rather modest to many others. In some states there may be widely differing views within the government and military bureaucracy. Although the disincentives will always seem important, they will not necessarily prevail. Credibly hinting at the capability or intention of acquiring nuclear weapons seems a more attractive strategy for several states than actually demonstrating possession. Since technical capacity and physical access to weapons materials can only increase, the opportunities for hinting will gradually become widespread.

The march of proliferation moves in only one direction. It is very unlikely that the world will have seen the end of the spread of nuclear weapons for the indefinite future. But one of the major dangers of proliferation is that its pace will outstrip the world's ability to adjust. Each new entry into the nuclear club would create a local, regional, or global instability. During the transition period until a new power equilibrium is reached, there would be an increased danger of conventional or nuclear warfare, particularly at the regional level. Disequilibrium might result in a series of regional arms races and perhaps accelerate the pace of proliferation. If enough states go nuclear in rapid succession, the ability of international systems to adjust might be swamped. The greater danger, of course, is escalation to widespread nuclear conflagration. Given a sufficiently modest rate of proliferation, however, or a preference among governments for hinting at rather than demonstrating capability, the world's institutions and political relationships might well be able to adjust, thus keeping the threat of instability and nuclear war small.

What can be said about the likely rate of nuclear proliferation? Any judgment given in the absence of a detailed, state-specific analysis of all near-nuclear states must necessarily be very tentative. With that reservation understood, the foregoing discussion suggests that the rate is likely to be quite slow. Although that conclusion is heartening, the range of uncertainty is large.

Many observers, of course, will not agree. They may in fact conclude the very opposite, that nuclear proliferation is likely to proceed quickly, thereby creating an unstable and dangerous world. Indeed, it is easy to find alarmists about proliferation. And though their position cannot be disproven, the preceding discussion may have rendered it less plausible. The actual rate of proliferation is intrinsically unpredictable. Some influences are difficult to discover or depend on unknowable future events. But several can be identified and are worth evaluating.

The rate of nuclear proliferation will depend, first, on the strength of the "positive feedback system" that seems to exist between one state's actions and another's. One state's going nuclear is likely to stimulate another to do the same. This reaction may result from neighboring or regional states' concern over security or political relationships. It may result also from a sense of inevitability, a state of mind created by a demonstrated failure to hold the line. Such an attitude is quite prevalent today, largely as a result of the Indian explosion and despite the fact that only its timing was really a surprise to informed observers.

Second, the rate will depend also on whether or not nuclear weapons are actually used. Yet the nature of this influence is uncertain. An explosion that killed few people and resulted in major political gains might stimulate proliferation. In contrast, one that killed thousands or hundreds of thousands or more and that occurred during a conventional war involving a new nuclear state might well have the opposite effect. The outcome of either scenario, though, cannot be predicted. Too many features unique to the particular circumstances would contribute to structuring the resultant psychological environment.

Third, the speed of diffusion of civilian nuclear power may affect the rate. Technical and economic barriers will decline as nuclear technology is introduced to more nations. Some observers claim that easier access to nuclear material will itself serve as an incentive to develop weapons. It seems more likely, however, that the effect will come in another way— namely, by lowering disincentives. Of course, the difference is not significant if the result is the same; but for planning a strategy for nonproliferation, it does in fact matter. A decline in technical and economic disincentives can be compensated for by a replacement with political and institutional ones. Thus the rate of proliferation may indeed remain quite independent of the rate at which nuclear technology is diffused.

Fourth, the rate will certainly depend on how individual governments weigh their incentives and disincentives. But that is an empty statement. What is actually needed is an understanding of governments' internal decision-making processes: how each will balance incentives and disincentives, which will be most important to particular governments and under what circumstances, and what can be done to influence their perceptions. This analysis has not yet addressed these questions. It has dealt not so much with real states in the context of their actual environment as with idealized states in undifferentiated environments. In so doing, a variety of instruments have been identified for influencing the primary nuclear incentives and disincentives of states and non-state entities. Before going on to a more state-specific discussion, these are worth recapitulating in order to suggest a general strategy of nonproliferation.

The likelihood of non-state entities using a nuclear weapon is not large and is negatively correlated with their ability to obtain one; those most able to acquire weapons would probably use them, if at all, in a manner calculated to minimize destruction. The major danger seems to be nuclear threat, not use. Yet this optimistic assessment does not obviate the need for concern, particularly since a conclusion based on past experience has no certainty of future validity. Governments could try to eliminate the motivations at least of nationally oriented revolutionary groups to use nuclear weapons by accommodating their objectives. This approach is risky, however, because it opens the door to nuclear blackmail. In any case, a government's stance toward such a group will derive primarily from other political motives unconnected to nuclear potential. More important ways to deal with a non-state entity's latent nuclear threat are active suppression and the denial of access to material or weapons. But active suppression of individuals or groups who might be inclined to use nuclear terror is extremely difficult. It requires adequate intelligence and cooperation among governments. Moreover, it should not be pursued so far as to undermine personal freedoms in domestic societies. Denial of access is probably a more fruitful approach. It requires adequate physical security measures applied to all nuclear weapons and fissile material in the world. Cooperation among governments combined with the good offices and technical assistance of the IAEA would aid these efforts. If material were stolen, action to recover it and to apprehend those responsible would have to be taken immediately. As with other forms of terrorism, however, cooperation of all governments would be essential. Sanctuary for nuclear thieves or terrorists must be denied. An international convention for cooperation would be a very useful means of assisting states in all these activities.

For many states, the critical requirement if they are to decide against a nuclear program will be the continuance of strong alliances and security guarantees with the superpowers, particularly the United States. The overall credibility of American security guarantees to its allies, as well as many other individual commitments, can be weakened only at the peril of encouraging the "abandoned" government to acquire nuclear weapons. Where more general political and security requirements argue strongly for maintaining commitments, the choice will not be difficult. Where the maintenance of existing alliances seems to contradict rather than support overall foreign policy objectives—such as encouraging the replacement of repressive governments, pursuing the development of relations with the Soviet Union or China, or damping regional conventional arms races—the choice will be more difficult. Where consensus does not exist, indecisiveness itself may breed a feeling of insecurity. Unfortunately, the credibility of one guarantee will to some extent depend on American willingness to fulfill another.

Given the realities of United States domestic politics, extension of American security guarantees to many additional states seems unlikely through the 1980s. Nonetheless, in some particular instances in which other objectives are not adversely affected, specific states are willing, and the commonality of interests and the overall political relationship would make a guarantee credible, such an extension might be feasible and appropriate. Of course, from the vantage point only of nonproliferation goals, regional security problems could be as usefully handled by Soviet guarantees as by American ones. Westerners, however, might see the extension of Soviet guarantees as undesirable because of the continuing East-West competition. Soviets no doubt would see extension of the American alliance system as equally undesirable.

Where possible, security incentives should be reduced by addressing regional security concerns directly. Regional security arrangements and nuclear-free zones would be appropriate in a few areas, particularly Oceania and sub-Saharan Africa, and should not be prevented by disagreements over auxiliary (although, admittedly, to some states important) issues such as transit and foreign basing of nuclear weapons. In regions suffering from serious ongoing disputes, the first priority must be to resolve, defuse, or stabilize them. Access to adequate conventional weaponry may be essential for states experiencing serious threats. The problem of nuclear proliferation cannot be solved prior to or independently of the security problems of individual states. The superpowers should be prepared to play a role in settling regional disputes if their intervention would lead to progress. In rare instances in which a threat seemed likely to deter proliferation, a superpower could threaten or hint that it would supply nuclear weapons to an ally if its regional adversaries acquired nuclear weapons.

Maintaining and strengthening the international behavioral norm

113

proscribing the acquisition of nuclear weapons is important as a means of influencing the domestic debates that will precede any decision to develop a nuclear capability. A permissive psychological environment conditioned by a weakened norm or an expectation that frequent violation will eradicate it would strengthen the case of nuclear advocates and undermine the supporters of abstinence. In order to maintain the norm, the NPT system must be preserved and the IAEA's safeguard machinery must be credible. Although accession by additional states—particularly the three nuclear states and the several near-nuclear states that are not party—would strengthen the NPT system, none are likely to join for the foreseeable future.

Attention should therefore focus on preventing the NPT's erosion through withdrawal or violation as well as on other means of strengthening the behavioral norm. Any actions of individual governments or international organizations that would lend support, even rhetorical, to the proscription of nuclear proliferation would be welcome. New nuclear-free zones would be particularly useful. Closing the loophole regarding peaceful nuclear explosions and terminating their international endorsement would also help. These latter measures now depend primarily on the Soviet Union. Creating an international mechanism to provide PNE services would probably be counterproductive. The goal of extending the nuclear-use taboo to nuclear acquisition could be promoted by either a Security Council resolution similar to Resolution 255 or, as a second best alternative, a joint Soviet-American declaration indicating that a state's acquisition of nuclear weapons would create a serious threat to peace and security and thus require consultation concerning possible action.

Closely related to the strengthening of the norm proscribing proliferation is the replacement of technical and economic barriers to the acquisition of weapons material with institutional and political barriers to the manufacture of explosives. While diffusion of civilian nuclear technology is inevitable, it will, in all likelihood, also be gradual.

Actions can and should be taken to dissuade states from reprocessing and from acquiring fuel-cycle facilities that use or produce weapons-grade material. Uranium exploration and production facilities should be expanded. States should be encouraged to stockpile enriched fuel, and suppliers could offer to buy back spent fuel or to trade it for enriched uranium. Spent-fuel repositories should be created to offer an attractive alternative to reprocessing for waste disposal. Sole reliance on preventing reprocessing is bound to fail, however, and should be augmented by efforts to induce those states that insist on reprocessing to rely on external providers of services. Sufficient capacity for both enrichment and reprocessing should be constructed under multinational control or, more likely, in nuclear or low-risk non-nuclear states. The existence of competitive suppliers would guarantee secure, economical access to these services, untied to political constraints other than those relating to nonproliferation. In the reprocessing case, plutonium could be stored at the site and exchanged for enriched uranium or returned to the country of origin only under safeguards and as needed for reactor operation.

Even if such actions were taken, some modest number of states would still remain committed to acquiring sensitive fuel-cycle facilities. But if these actions are not taken, the number will be higher. Sensitive technology cannot be denied indefinitely to determined states, both because they can probably find some supplier and because, in most cases, they could develop it on their own. Thus supplier states could agree not to transfer sensitive technology and still not have a significant impact on access to weapons-grade material.

For those states that cannot be persuaded to rely on others, their eagerness to purchase nuclear facilities and technology rather than develop them independently should be seen as an opportunity. Except for particular high-risk states, whose requests to purchase sensitive facilities should be denied, regulated transfer should govern the management of the international nuclear industry. Under this philosophy, the sale or transfer of nuclear fuel-cycle facilities would be associated with solemn pledges to accept safeguards; to forswear the right to use materials, equipment, or technology obtained for explosives purposes; to refrain from transferring to third parties without comparable guarantees; and to provide adequate physical protection. If the international nuclear industry expanded in this regulated fashion, the norm proscribing proliferation would be greatly strengthened and diversion would become quite unlikely. Regulated transfer cannot guarantee that no diversion would occur, but neither could any other approach. Bilateral and international political assurances are not given lightly by governments and are not easily ignored or reversed. Relying on these and strengthening them with appropriate institutional arrangements and operating procedures is the most feasible way to manage the industry.

Proliferation is primarily a political and psychological problem and should be confronted with appropriate political and institutional instruments. Attempting to deny access to technology against the wishes of governments is a strategy doomed to failure or guaranteed to be very costly in terms of other objectives.

Little, if anything, can be done to reduce the actual significance of nuclear weapons for global and regional power relationships. But the prestige and symbolic importance of nuclear weapons can be reduced. The importance of other political assets could be recognized explicitly by the broadening of the membership of various international decision-making bodies to include additional non-nuclear states. Superpower arms control—particularly a comprehensive test ban, but to some extent SALT agreements and perhaps a no-use declaration against non-nuclear states—would be marginally useful if negotiations were not so prolonged that the symbolic importance of nuclear weapons was more emphasized by the process than reduced by the outcome. To the extent that disputes involving nuclear powers can be settled without resort to explicit nuclear threats, the apparent importance of nuclear weapons would be further diminished. American government officials should also take more care to minimize the extent to which their public statements reinforce the nuclear ambitions of non-nuclear states.

Means should also be sought, when conflict with other important values or objectives is lacking or minor, to accommodate ambitions that might tempt governments to acquire nuclear weapons. This is a difficult and risky business. Weakness in confronting overt blackmail does not solve the problem; in fact, it only invites more blackmail. The case is less clear-cut with respect to the subtle forms of pressure that are more likely. These must simply be judged on their own merits. Transferring significant wealth and economic power to certain states and recognizing their world position or hegemonial role probably would reduce their immediate incentives to acquire nuclear weapons but might well increase their long-term ambitions.

Using the threat of military or severe economic sanctions as a means of dissuading potential proliferators is not desirable for both pragmatic and normative reasons. The threat of intervention would not only damage political relationships but also probably not be credible except in very special cases. Soviet intervention into an Eastern European state, for example, might well be believable. But the expected political or military costs or the risk of great-power confrontation would generally be too high. Severe economic sanctions applied to a nation that acquired weapons would be useful only as an example to other states. If imposed successfully (which is highly unlikely), they would be a heavy penalty to inflict for a very uncertain benefit. Moreover, since new nuclear states cannot be made to disappear except by drastic military action, the ultimate results of severe economic sanctions might well be more damaging than constructive. The rapid imposition of relatively minor and symbolic but highly visible and emotive sanctions would help prevent the impression that other governments are indifferent to proliferation or that it is costless. More useful still, of course, would be moral suasion exerted before governments crossed the nuclear threshold. Such influence can most usefully be exercised between a superpower and its clients and allies.

A general strategy for nonproliferation can now be summarized as follows:

- Maintaining or strengthening existing security guarantees and extending them when appropriate
- Working to resolve or stabilize regional disputes that might stimulate proliferation
- Strengthening the international behavioral norm proscribing the acquisition of nuclear weapons
- Acting through the international nuclear market to dissuade states from acquiring their own sensitive nuclear facilities
- Replacing technical and economic barriers against access to weapons materials with institutional and political barriers against using them to make weapons
- Reducing the prestige and symbolic importance of nuclear weapons in world politics
- In special cases, satisfying some of the ambitions of potential nuclear states or non-state entities
- Applying moral suasion to potential proliferators and minor sanctions to those who acquire weapons
- Physically protecting weapons and weapons material
- Actively suppressing nuclear-prone non-state entities

117

One or another combination of these instruments cannot be recommended for use in a particular circumstance without several reservations. First, there are some incentives and disincentives that are not easily influenced. These include any arising from a general political conflict, a regional competition, or the division of the world into nuclear and non-nuclear states. To the extent that these dominate a state's calculation, the application of available instruments by other states or the international community may be of little value. Second, the use of any of these instruments in order to inhibit nuclear proliferation will frequently contend with other important objectives. For instance, decisions about whether to use conventional arms transfers in order to maintain or strengthen alliance relationships and to provide non-nuclear alternatives for a state's security needs frequently involve such a conflict. Therefore any decision to pursue a particular approach must depend on a more general analysis involving a broader set of concerns. Third, a given action or policy can act to inhibit proliferation in one case yet stimulate it in another. Worse, it can sometimes have both effects simultaneously on different groups within one nation. Moral suasion applied through an alliance system, for example, may persuade one faction to refrain from seeking nuclear capability and another—that may see the effort to persuade as proof of a weakening alliance—to try even harder to attain weapons. Thus the impact of a particular policy instrument, either in general or on a particular state, can be impossible to predict. With these reservations in mind, this analysis will conclude by briefly examining the application of the suggested strategy to four categories of states.

One group includes Israel, South Africa, South Korea, and Taiwan. These states all are currently (or, in the case of South Korea, could soon be) so severely challenged by others that the legitimacy of their borders or governments or their very existence as sovereign nations is in question. Such threats may provide strong nuclear incentives. They would not acquire nuclear weapons primarily with the intention of using them, but rather as a means of altering political relationships in a way that would reduce their adversaries' challenges. These states all have sufficient resources and technical capacity to develop nuclear weapons in a relatively few years. Indeed, many people already consider Israel to be a full-fledged nuclear state even though it has never detonated an explosive. They are all sufficiently isolated within the international community that the norm proscribing proliferation may have little or no effect. With the exclusion of South Korea, that has in the past had revisionist ambitions toward North Korea and may have them again, their primary motive is only to preserve their sovereignty and governments. The most desirable way to restrain nuclear ambitions in each case would be to resolve the dispute and to alleviate the challenge. The security problems of none of these states seem imminently amenable to such a solution, however.

For South Korea and Taiwan, the most useful instruments of a nonproliferation strategy seem to be maintainence or strengthening of the credibility of American security guarantees, combined with careful and selective applicaton of moral suasion by the United States. There are difficulties, however. First and perhaps most important is the possibility that confidence in American willingness to fulfill its security obligations will gradually erode. Second is the conflict between maintaining these alliance relations and achieving other objectives: the evolution of the governments to less repressive and more democratic regimes and, in the case of Taiwan, full normalization of relations with China. China no doubt recognizes the possibility of Taiwan's going nuclear and may somewhat moderate its behavior in order to reduce that likelihood. Third, the exercise of moral suasion (as in the persuasion of South Korea to forego its reprocessing plant) might ultimately be counterproductive by strengthening some domestic proponents of the nuclear option. Since both states are parties to the NPT, all their civilian nuclear facilities will be under IAEA safeguard. Agreements accompanying the sale of nuclear facilities to these countries would reinforce and strengthen the effect of the NPT. Nevertheless, Taiwan and South Korea might well be states to which sensitive nuclear technology should not be transferred under any condition.

Israel's concern about stimulating nuclear programs in neighboring states and the risk that any future Middle East war could escalate to nuclear levels act as very strong disincentives. They have probably been the major reasons underlying Israel's reluctance to claim officially a nuclear capability, if not preventing it from actually acquiring one. Israel may currently see itself as being in an ideal position with respect to nuclear capability. It reaps most of the political benefits but pays few of the costs. Thus efforts to prevent Israel's using nuclear weapons are more important than those directed against acquisition. Ultimately, this task requires averting a situation in which Israel's destruction is imminent, and preferably, altogether reducing the likelihood of war. Superpower mediation or intervention during a Middle East war and the availability of conventional weaponry have an obvious relevance here.

The South African case is almost as complex. South Africa's perception of black African states' militancy will influence its decisions. At present it appears to be gradually adopting a policy, similar to Israel's, of credible hinting. Although an American security treaty would certainly reduce South Africa's nuclear incentives, it would conflict directly with other American objectives in Africa. The South African case is indeed a dilemma. Perhaps the only leverage available is moral suasion on the part of the United States and its European allies, on whom South Africa does strongly—but not decisively—depend. The cost of preventing a nuclear South Africa, or at least one that is very close to a nuclear capability, might have to be acceptance of the current regime's legitimacy.

Another group of potential nuclear states includes India, Japan, Iran, Brazil, Indonesia, Iraq, Algeria, Nigeria, and perhaps Zaire. (India, of course, has already detonated its first explosive, but there is some question about what it will do in the future.) These states either currently or might eventually aspire to regional or global status or leadership in the Third World. Some may come to believe that nuclear weapons are a necessary step in that quest. Security problems, while not their primary motivation, are important to some. Tempering the symbolic and prestige value of having nuclear weapons and arranging non-nuclear means of satisfying their ambitions would be the most effective means of reducing their incentives. Japan, for example, has achieved a status slightly below the superpowers simply by virtue of its economic strength. Iran and Algeria have gained stature through their oil. Algeria has also attained some recognition as a Third World leader. Brazil may be on its way to achieving a dominant position in South America. The reluctance to encourage neighbors to acquire nuclear weapons is already an important disincentive. Other disincentives can be created through regulated nuclear transfers and by strengthening the international norm proscribing proliferation. A nuclear-free zone in sub-Saharan Africa has obvious utility. Japan, Indonesia, Iran, Nigeria, and Zaire are already parties to the NPT. Moral suasion should also be employed whenever possible and necessary.

A third group of states includes Pakistan, Australia, Syria, and perhaps Egypt. The fundamental existence of these nations is not in jeopardy, and they do not really have ambitions for leadership and status that nuclear weapons might aid (although Egypt does aspire to be a leader within the Arab League). However, their security concerns or political competition with neighboring or regional states may make them feel compelled to acquire a nuclear arsenal. Pakistan's actions would be responsive to India's and perhaps Iran's, Australia's to Indonesia's, Syria's to Israel's or Iraq's, Egypt's to Israel's or Libya's. To the extent that security concerns are important, American guarantees significantly lower incentives for Pakistan and Australia. An American Middle East policy that suggested an intention to constrain Israel in the event of renewed warfare would do the same for Egypt. The incentives deriving from political competition can be minimized by a reduction in the prestige value and symbolic importance of nuclear weapons and by a reduction of each government's uncertainty about its adversary's intentions. Disincentives can be increased through moral suasion, a strengthened behavioral norm, and reliance on nuclear transfers to strengthen institutional and political barriers.

A fourth category of states currently is limited to Argentina, did include France during the 1950s, and could eventually encompass others. This group is defined not by primary motivation but by the great independence and ability of the governments' atomic energy establishments to move their nations toward nuclear capability. Indeed, if classified according to motivation, France belongs with states seeking global status; Argentina's interests are to recapture its once-dominant position in South America and to respond to or perhaps anticipate Brazil's actions. Where a strong bureaucracy has its own ambitions not necessarily related to national interests, actions could respond to its particular incentives. While the utility of various actions would vary from case to case, possible approaches would again include strengthening the norm against proliferation, reducing the apparent value of nuclear weapons, creating political and institutional barriers through nuclear transfers, and accommodating by non-nuclear means the ambitions of the nuclear proponents. Especially in this case, direct or indirect intervention in the domestic politics of the potential proliferants might be useful in reducing the likelihood that nuclear proponents will prevail.

This brief review has done no more than merely illustrate how the various instruments of a strategy for nonproliferation can be combined into an overall policy. No single instrument is likely to be totally effective alone. Each state will require an approach tailored to its own situation. There is no simple or guaranteed formula for restricting proliferation. So, too, there is nothing to be gained by ignoring either the close linkage between nuclear incentives and continuing interstate military and political conflict or the evidence that nuclear weapons are important sources, symbols, and instruments of national power. These fundamental facts must be recognized and taken into account if nuclear proliferation is to be halted or, more likely, kept to a slow enough pace that will allow gradual adjustment.

Alternative Strategies for International Control of Nuclear Power

Harold A. Feiveson and Theodore B. Taylor

ONE

Overview

The Problem

The spread and development of civilian nuclear power is exposing a rising and potentially staggering amount of plutonium to the risk of diversion for use in nuclear weapons. Without new national and international actions by the 1980s, many nations will be drifting toward possession of nuclear weapons and to fuel cycles vulnerable to theft of plutonium by terrorists or other criminals. Through the fog of controversy over the future of nuclear power, it is this risk of diversion of fissle material for weapons purposes that appears to raise the issues most difficult to resolve and most insistently fundamental to the way people feel about nuclear power. These are the issues that we believe ought to decide the character of the next stage in the development of nuclear power in the United States and abroad. This study evaluates alternative futures for nuclear power explicitly from the standpoint of how the spread of nuclear weapons might be curbed.

One aspect of these issues on which we focus attention in this analysis is latent proliferation. Most people seem to worry about what is traditionally called the *proliferation* of nuclear weapons, that is, the demonstrated acquisition of usable nuclear weapons by nations or criminals. But there are degrees of drift or concerted action toward the actual possession of nuclear explosives that can be used for destructive purposes. We use the phrase latent proliferation to include those degrees that fall short of actual diversion of nuclear materials from civilian nuclear facilities but facilitate a possible future decision to acquire nuclear weapons. The time and resources required to make the transition from a condition of latent to one of demonstrated proliferation also range from very large to very small. Inadequate control of stockpiles of concentrated plutonium separated from spent fuel, combined with the knowledge of how to design and fabricate a nuclear explosive and the possession of tested non-nuclear components of nuclear weapons, can allow a nation or a criminal group to have nuclear weapons within days of even hours after diverting or overtly stealing a dozen or so kilograms of the plutonium. This situation can be contrasted with that of a nation that has nuclear power plants but no facilities for enriching uranium or separating plutonium from nuclear reactor fuel. It would be much further away from actually having nuclear weapons and inherently much better protected from theft of plutonium by criminals.

The Once-through Fuel Cycle

The present stage of nuclear power development is dominated by the deployment of essentially two reactor technologies: light-water reactors (fueled by slightly enriched uranium), pioneered in the United States and now also being produced by industrial combines in France, West Germany, Japan, Sweden, and the Soviet Union; and the heavy-water CANDU reactor (fueled by unenriched uranium), produced for domestic and export markets by a joint industry-government venture in Canada. Both reactor technologies currently use a once-through fuel cycle that progresses from the uranium enrichment plant (in the case of light-water reactors), to the fuel fabrication plant, to the reactor, to spent-fuel storage. Nowhere in this fuel cycle does there exist weapons-grade material (that is material from which fission explosives can be made without isotope enrichment)—plutonium or the separated ^{233}U and ^{235}U isotopes of uranium—*except in the spent fuel,* where the plutonium produced in reactors is mixed with highly radioactive fission waste products and large quantities of ^{238}U, the abundant isotope of natural uranium. Nowhere in this fuel cycle is there need to isolate and work with the highly toxic isotopes of plutonium.

Despite the simplicity of the once-through fuel cycle, many observers believe that it cannot form the basis for a mature and stable nuclear industry. If the growth rate of nuclear power is sufficiently small, a once-through system can probably be designed to last several decades. But it is a system that is destined to exhaust estimated high-grade worldwide reserves of uranium in a matter of decades. For this reason, the long-term vitality of fission power is generally believed to depend on the introduction of breeder reactors that can convert the abundant fertile material, ^{238}U or thorium, into the chain-reacting nuclear fuels, plutonium or ^{233}U. Such conversion could expand the resource base for nuclear fission over 100 times. Eventually nuclear fission systems must begin to evolve into such regenerative breeder cycles or be phased out altogether.

The Phase-out Option

The effects of a phase-out of fission power are dependent on the availability of alternative sources of energy. The major long-term possibilities are coal; fusion; geothermal energy from hot, dry rock; and solar energy.

Coal is so unevenly distributed that many countries would have to depend on long-term, secure trade arrangements with other countries if it were to be a primary source of their energy. Its combustion products, furthermore, may cause unacceptable climatic changes if we continue to use it on a large scale and can be a serious health hazard now. The health hazard may be controllable in the future.

Much attention is now being directed toward the possibility of harnessing fusion, the process used in hydrogen bombs, as a source of energy for peaceful purposes. The future of fusion is technically and economically uncertain. Successful development of fusion would also provide an alternative route to nuclear weapons, since economically attractive fusion power plants could also provide relatively cheap neutrons for converting natural uranium or thorium to fission weapon materials. This risk is related to a possible opportunity: the use of fusion neutrons to convert thorium to ^{233}U for use in reactors that are not quite able to breed more nuclear fuel than they consume (*converter reactors*). It is quite possible that fusion may become economically attractive for this purpose before it is competitive for direct production of electric power or usable thermal energy.

The potential reserves of usable geothermal energy in hot, dry rock are huge and widely distributed. The economics of using such sources are uncertain, however, as are a number of environmental effects associated with air and water pollution and seismic phenomena. If used on a large scale, this source of energy is not renewable in any practical sense: the rate of heating of accessible rock by radioactive decay of materials in the earth's crust is orders of magnitude smaller than would be required to sustain a practical rate of removal of heat from the rock.

Solar energy is abundant, renewable, widely distributed, but diffuse. Even if used on a large scale, the collection and subsequent conversion of solar energy to other forms of energy could, with appropriate technology, result in much less damaging side effects than would the use of any other prospective energy source. Significant regional changes in the earth's heat balance can be avoided if collection systems are widely distributed and designed so as to avoid significant changes in the regional reflectivity of the surface. The prospective performance and economics of solar energy systems for space heating and cooling; production of clean, combustible fuels; and production of electricity are so uncertain, however, as to cause considerable controversy. Some observers argue that much more intensive efforts to develop and commercialize solar energy systems could make them the world's primary source of energy within a few decades. Others argue that high capital costs for all applications except space and hot water heating in ideal locations will keep the cost of usable solar energy much higher than costs of energy from nuclear sources or coal. We are more optimistic about solar energy than most people and are encouraged by the increasing rate at which promising new concepts are being proposed and assessed. The biggest uncertainty about solar energy, in our minds, is how long it will take to implement its use on a large scale. However, it is not at all clear that this time will be significantly longer than the time required to develop worldwide fission breeder reactor systems that are effectively safeguarded against diversion of nuclear materials to destructive purposes.

The Plutonium Breeder Option

The path that the worldwide nuclear industry appears most clearly determined to follow is to separate the plutonium contained in spent reactor fuel and to recycle it as fresh fuel, first into light-water reactors and later into fast plutonium breeders. Commercial reprocessing of spent reactor fuel may soon be possible in several countries: the United Kingdom, France, West Germany, India, Japan, the Soviet Union, and the United States. Still other countries including Argentina, Brazil,

Italy, Pakistan, Spain, and Yugoslavia, have announced plans to deploy their own reprocessing plants. The United Kingdom, France, West Germany, Japan, the Soviet Union, and the United States also have significant programs of breeder development under way, all of them focused on a single technology: the liquid-metal fast plutonium assembly. The crucial disadvantage of these developments is that they introduce the troublesome element plutonium into a central position in nuclear commerce. This disadvantage is compounded by a marked lack of clarity and consensus on how the plutonium should be safeguarded against national and criminal diversion to weapons purposes.

Nuclear power systems based on the ^{238}U-plutonium breeding cycle require that weapons-grade plutonium be separated from spent fuel and incorporated into fresh fuel for recycling in power reactors. If the nuclear power plants are nationally owned and operated, this cycle necessarily provides all nations using it with potential access to plutonium for production of nuclear weapons. In principle, national access to plutonium could be avoided by the production of all nuclear power in multinationally owned and operated regional centers that exported electricity. But this possibility is unlikely to be politically or economically acceptable to countries that would then be dependent on electric power sources beyond their borders. Even if all plutonium were separated and refabricated in internationally controlled, heavily guarded regional centers—an often-discussed alternative—the risk of criminal theft of plutonium in fresh fuel in transit or storage at power plants would persist.

Because the plutonium path is consonant with present plans of worldwide nuclear industries and initially requires no major new international agreements or novel departures of national policy, it looks relatively simple and practical compared with the alternatives. But this superficial simplicity is deceptive. The drift to a plutonium economy, unchecked, will by the 1980s place weapons-grade materials in the hands of many countries and will further require an increasing intensity of control over this material within each country to protect the material against theft by criminals and terrorists. Attempts to safeguard the plutonium against national diversion will lead step by step to cumbersome and complex international control systems. Strong security measures to protect plutonium against theft worldwide will be difficult to implement without major infringements of national sovereignty. In some countries, such measures may also lead to excessive use of paramilitary guard forces and other severe security measures.

The Thorium Option

The use of large quantities of thorium instead of uranium in reactors would also permit a fuel regeneration system, but one in which the uranium isotope ^{233}U rather than plutonium would be the key link in making further use of spent reactor fuel. Power systems based primarily on the thorium-^{233}U breeding cycle (hereafter referred to simply as the "thorium cycle") could be established in such a way that fresh fuel supplied to national reactors would contain no weapons-grade material. The reason such a possibility exists for the thorium cycle is that ^{233}U can be diluted (*denatured*) with the naturally abundant isotope ^{238}U to such an extent that the uranium would be unusable, without isotope separation, as nuclear explosives material. No such denaturing isotope of plutonium will exist in significant quantities. This possible form of a thorium cycle has not, to our knowledge, been previously explored from a nuclear weapons proliferation perspective.

The fresh fuel at national reactors would consist of a mixture of roughly 1 part ^{233}U, about 8 parts ^{238}U, and twenty to eighty parts thorium, depending on the type of reactor. Present types of reactors (both light-water and heavy-water) could be converted to operate on this fuel mixture. The 8 to 1 ratio of ^{238}U to ^{233}U would be sufficient, for practical purposes, to denature the uranium so that it could not be used for nuclear explosives unless the fuel mixture underwent isotope enrichment, a process much more difficult and costly than the chemical separation of plutonium. The denatured uranium, both in the fresh fuel assemblies and in the spent fuel, would thus not be weapons-grade. There would be some plutonium in the spent fuel,[1] but much less than in a uranium-plutonium breeding cycle.

The fabrication of the fresh fuel assemblies and any necessary denaturing of the ^{233}U could be done at internationally controlled, regional reprocessing and reactor centers. Such centers would also undertake whatever reprocessing of spent fuel from the thorium reactors would be required. The regional reprocessing centers would, of course, require physical security against theft of plutonium by criminals or terrorists.

[1]Neutron capture by the ^{238}U dilutant would yield plutonium.

But fresh fuels shipped to national power plants and spent fuel shipped back to the regional centers would not be attractive targets for theft: the fresh fuel would not be of weapons grade, and the spent fuel would be so highly radioactive and so diluted as to be effectively self-protecting against theft and the subsequent processing required to make nuclear explosives.

It is unlikely that current types of nuclear power plants could breed sufficient amounts of ^{233}U to be self-sustaining on a thorium cycle if the recycled ^{233}U were denatured with ^{238}U. But they could be part of an overall system that was self-sustaining if some additional source of ^{233}U could be provided at the same internationally controlled regional centers at which the fuel were reprocessed. One possibility for supplementing the ^{233}U in the cycle would be fast breeder reactors that used plutonium extracted from the converter reactor fuels and thorium as the "fertile material" for producing ^{233}U. Such reactors could produce more ^{233}U than the plutonium they consumed. All recycled plutonium could be consumed on-site at the regional centers, so that the need for any national access to plutonium would be avoided.

Another, more speculative possibility is to use fusion reactors at the regional centers primarily to produce excess neutrons that would convert thorium into the ^{233}U needed to keep the entire nuclear power system self-sustaining. In this case, regional reactors could be used to consume plutonium produced in the nationally operated converter reactors serviced by the regional facilities. Both of these possibilities are discussed below in more detail.

Our preliminary study of the thorium cycle has shown that its characteristics depend *very* strongly on the assumed rate of nuclear power growth and on the assumed timing of changeover from the present to the new fuel cycle. In general, the economics and room for flexibility in the cycle look more attractive for low than for high projections of nuclear power growth rates.

The Necessity to Assess the Options

We should make it clear that we do not view the thorium cycle or even a complete phase-out of civilian nuclear power as alternatives (to the plutonium economy) that would remove the risks of nuclear weapon proliferation. Huge quantities of nuclear materials suitable for military purposes—and, of course, nuclear weapons themselves—will still have to be securely protected from theft. Furthermore, pressures for nations to acquire nuclear weapons will persist at least as long as the nuclear weapons states continue to behave as though they feel more secure with nuclear weapons than without them. We see no practical way technically to *prevent* any nation that really wants nuclear weapons from acquiring them. Material for weapons can be extracted from natural uranium by isotope enrichment, which, though now very difficult and costly, is likely to become easier soon. More serious still, the technical know-how and basic materials required for indigenous plutonium production and reprocessing are accessible to any country with a strong resolve to use them. Nor will a shift to any type of fission fuel cycle prevent nations from using their civilian power reactors to produce plutonium, albeit in violation of agreements, for subsequent extraction in reprocessing facilities built specifically for yielding plutonium for nuclear weapons.

It is clear also that no alternative fission future will be an easy path to follow. In particular, there are a great number of unresolved technical and institutional issues involved in implementation of a thorium cycle; we do not presume that upon further analysis the thorium option will necessarily look very attractive, either from a proliferation or other perspectives. Rather, we wish to make the case that given certain attractive reactor engineering characteristics of a thorium cycle and the fact that ^{233}U and ^{235}U can be denatured whereas plutonium cannot, the present worldwide momentum toward a uranium-plutonium breeding cycle in preference to a thorium option should at least be thoroughly reexamined before irreversible commitments are made to the plutonium economy. The additional research and development expenditures that would be involved in such reexamination are minute compared with the projected nuclear investments over the next two decades or to the incalculable dangers of the spread of nuclear weapons to many more countries.

It will take considerable time and effort to assess the three alternative fission futures we discuss in this paper—a uranium-plutonium cycle, a thorium cycle, and an orderly phase-out of fission power—and then implement whatever energy policy is determined to be in the best interests of each country and the world as a whole. The world has, we are convinced, the resources required for this task. And the world can substantially extend the time needed to consider and decide which new paths to follow by seizing the many opportunities now available for conserving energy produced by present types of power systems.

The primary conclusion we have drawn from this examination of fundamental energy options for the 1980s and beyond is this: Plutonium should not be separated from spent fuel from civilian reactors anywhere in the world until at least the two alternatives to a plutonium economy that we have sketched above have been thoroughly evaluated and compared with a worldwide plutonium economy safeguarded as effectively as is practically possible against diversion of plutonium for destructive purposes.

Outline of the Monograph

The line of our argument is straightforward. We hold that:

- Without major new international initiatives to impose safeguards on civilian nuclear power, the hazards of criminal and national diversion of plutonium to destructive uses will markedly increase.
- To impede this dangerous drift, it is possible to formulate a few practical guidelines for the establishment of an effective international safeguards system.
- A plutonium economy cannot, without extraordinary difficulty and contrivance, be made to conform to these guidelines.
- A thorium cycle has certain marked advantages, with respect to these guidelines, over a uranium-plutonium cycle.
- The thorium cycle, nuclear fission phase-out, or other options should not be prematurely foreclosed by a haphazard drift toward a plutonium economy.
- Any economic and technological penalties paid by the United States and the rest of the world for delaying the extraction and recycle of plutonium for approximately a decade are likely to be small compared with the benefits of thoroughly exploring and, where indicated, implementing any of the alternatives we discuss in this paper and other options that surely will be identified during that period.

None of the choices for meeting the world's increasing demands for

133

energy is either risk-free or easy to implement. All would require radically new national and international actions if a generally acceptable balance between risks and benefits is to be determined by the forces of reason rather than the inertia of past decisions and trends. But we owe it to ourselves and to our descendants to do the best we can to determine what these actions should be and how best to implement them.

TWO

The Safeguards Challenge

The essence of the security dilemma posed by civilian nuclear power is that the primary nuclear fuels—plutonium and the ^{235}U and ^{233}U isotopes of uranium—that can produce energy inside a power reactor can also be used for making nuclear explosives if obtained in sufficient quantity and concentration. Our focus is therefore on safeguards against diversion of these fuels from civilian nuclear power systems to the construction of nuclear explosives.

There are two types of diversion to be safeguarded against: diversion by criminals for terrorist or other purposes and diversion by nations. We consider the former first, not necessarily because we believe it poses greater dangers but because its dangers are more evidently universal. Theft of weapons-grade materials from any country's nuclear facilities would cause considerable national and international concern, whether or not that country already had nuclear weapons.

With respect to national diversion, we shall, as noted in Chapter One, emphasize the process of latent proliferation, that is, actions taken prior to the deliberate diversion of nuclear materials from civilian nuclear power channels which could accelerate the process of acquiring nuclear weapons *after* diversion had taken place. Such actions could include, for example, stockpiling of nuclear weapons materials in forms that could be quickly converted for use in nuclear weapons or the design, construction, and testing of the non-nuclear components of nuclear explosives before any actual diversion had taken place.

THEFT BY CRIMINALS

There is some dispute concerning the precise difficulty and hazards involved in the design and actual fabrication of nuclear explosives once the required amounts of weapons-grade nuclear materials are in the hands of a criminal or terrorist group. Nevertheless, there is growing evidence that this possibility is taken very seriously by responsible authorities in the United States and several other countries that now have substantial quantities of these materials.[2]

The basic knowledge required for the design and construction of highly destructive fission explosives is available in widely published, authoritative articles and books and is shared by thousands of people who have worked on nuclear explosives in the nations that have demonstrably built them. It is our conviction that given the required amount of fission-product-free plutonium, highly enriched uranium, or ^{233}U, it is quite conceivable that a criminal or terrorist group, or even one person working alone, could design and build a crude fission bomb that could be carried in a small automobile and would be likely to explode with a yield equivalent to at least 100 tons of high explosive.

The performance and reliability of such devices made with plutonium extracted from present types of nuclear power reactor spent fuels would depend on the knowledge and skills of the criminal group and on the chemical and isotopic composition of the plutonium. But all isotopes of plutonium produced in significant quantities in present and planned types of nuclear power plants could be used, separately or in combination, as the core material for highly destructive fission explosives.

[2]See the following: U. S. Atomic Energy Commision, *Technical Report WASH-1535, Proposed Final Environmental Statement, Liquid Metal Fast Breeder Reactor Program,* Washington, D.C., 1974; David M. Rosenbaum et al., *Special Safeguards Study,* prepared for the Atomic Energy Commission's Director of Licensing, spring 1974; Mason Willrich and Theodore B. Taylor, *Nuclear Theft; Risks and Safeguards,* Ballinger, Cambridge, Mass., 1974; Comptroller General of the United States, *Improvements Needed in the Program for the Protection of Special Nuclear Materials,* report to the Congress, November 1973; General Accounting Office, *Protecting Special Nuclear Materials in Transit: Improvements Made and Existing Problems* (B-184105), Report to the Congress, 1974; John McPhee, *The Curve of Binding Energy,* Farrar, Straus & Giroux, New York, 1974; and The Stanley Foundation, *Nuclear Theft and Terrorism,* report on Sixteenth Strategy for Peace Conference, October 1975.

Furthermore, the plutonium does not necessarily have to be in metallic form for this purpose. Plutonium oxide, for example, in the form that plutonium would have after separation and conversion at a fuel reprocessing plant, could also be used; the amount of plutonium required for the same performance of the explosive would be greater than if it were in metallic form.[3]

It is much easier to make fission bombs with yields reliably in the range of several kilotons to several dozen kilotons, using uranium enriched to substantially more than 20 percent in the isotope ^{235}U, or concentrated ^{233}U, than it is using plutonium of the type produced in present types of commercial nuclear power plants. The reason for this is that the plutonium produced in present types of light-water or heavy-water reactors contains considerable quantities of the isotope ^{240}Pu, which spontaneously fissions, releasing neutrons that can start a chain reaction before a nuclear explosive device has been fully assembled. This design difficulty is much alleviated when highly enriched uranium or ^{233}U is used as the nuclear explosive core material, since they represent much smaller sources of neutrons than do present types of power-reactor plutonium. But we should emphasize that the yields highly likely to be achievable with relatively crude plutonium bombs, though substantially less than the yield of the Hiroshima weapon (about 15 kilotons), are nevertheless sufficient, if detonated in especially densely populated areas, to kill 100,000 or more people.[4]

The quantities of weapons-grade materials needed by a criminal group for illicit construction of fission bombs would depend on the type and chemical composition of the materials to be used and on the knowledge, skills, and intentions of the group. Under many conceivable circumstances, the amounts of plutonium or ^{233}U required for relatively crude devices would be roughly a dozen kilograms and two or three times this amount if the material were highly enriched uranium.[5]

Given that it is credible that criminal groups could design and build fission bombs with stolen weapons-grade materials, we must ask

[3]David Hall, "The Adaptability of Fissile Materials to Nuclear Explosives" in R. B. Leachman and P. Althoff, (eds.), *Preventing Nuclear Theft: Guidelines for Industry and Government,* Praeger Publications, New York, 1972; see also Willrich and Taylor, *Nuclear Theft,* p. 13.

[4]Willrich and Taylor, *Nuclear Theft,* p. 22.

[5]Ibid., p. 16.

whether it is credible that such groups might actually want to use nuclear explosives to serve their purposes.[6] The threat of nuclear retaliation, which many observers consider to be the primary deterrent against nuclear attacks by nations, would generally not affect a terrorist or ciminal organization as it would a national government, with territory and a civilian population to protect. In many conceivable situations, the threatening organization need not identify itself to achieve large-scale disorder or to force compliance with its demands. Furthermore, the organization's members are likely to be dispersed within the general population. Ironically, small extremist groups may be invulnerable to the nuclear counterthreats that hold the world's superpowers at bay.

The qualitatively greater destructive power of nuclear explosives than of conventional arms or explosives and the widespread public fear of the effects of nuclear radiation offer potential opportunities for coercion or outright destruction on much bigger scales than have characterized terrorist or criminal acts in the past. For example, a criminal group not necessarily with established extremist political ambitions might distribute several small nuclear explosives in heavily populated areas and then issue a public threat to detonate the explosives one by one unless certain severe demands were met. Thus nuclear explosives might give an alienated group an extremely powerful lever to use against society if it were willing to go to such extremes.

Nuclear explosives are not the only weapons of mass destruction that might be used by criminals or terrorists in the future. There are a host of biological and chemical warfare agents, for example, that could also be used for such purposes and that require less effort than stealing nuclear weapons materials and making illicit nuclear bombs. But explosives, not poisons, have so far been the primary tools for large-scale destruction by terrorists or blackmailers. We cannot be sure this will be the case in the future. But we argue strongly that whatever patterns of criminal behavior may develop in the future, it would be foolish indeed to conclude that real threats or actual acts of nuclear violence by criminals or terrorists would not be credible *if* they could get their hands on the necessary nuclear materials.

At present, and for at least another decade or so, the amounts of

[6]Ted Greenwood's study in this volume addresses this question, as will subsequent work of the the 1980s Project on terrorism.

plutonium produced in the world's civilian power reactors are enormously greater than the quantities of highly enriched uranium (^{233}U) associated with such reactors. As far as we know, only one civilian power plant that uses highly enriched uranium[7] is now operating, and no others are under construction. It will produce substantial quantities of ^{233}U by conversion of thorium in the fuel, but no reprocessing of that fuel is now planned. All other operating or planned nuclear power plants operate on the ^{235}U-plutonium-^{238}U cycle, use no highly enriched uranium, and produce no ^{233}U.

Fortunately the once-through fuel cycle now used for nearly all nuclear power systems (depicted in Figure 1) possesses intrinsic safeguards against the theft of plutonium by criminal groups. First of all, fresh uranium fuel going into the reactors is much too diluted in ^{235}U (no more than 4 percent for light-water reactors; less than 1 percent for heavy-water reactors) to be used for nuclear weapons without further enrichment to substantially above 20 percent. We find it incredible that the technology for uranium enrichment, on the scale necessary to make at least one bomb in a year or so, could be acquired by a terrorist or criminal group for the foreseeable future. That is, the danger that such groups would themselves produce the explosive material for a uranium-type bomb is remote.

[7] A high-temperature, gas-cooled reactor (HTGR) at Fort St. Vrain, Colorado.

FIGURE 1

**Current
Once-through Fuel Cycle**

139

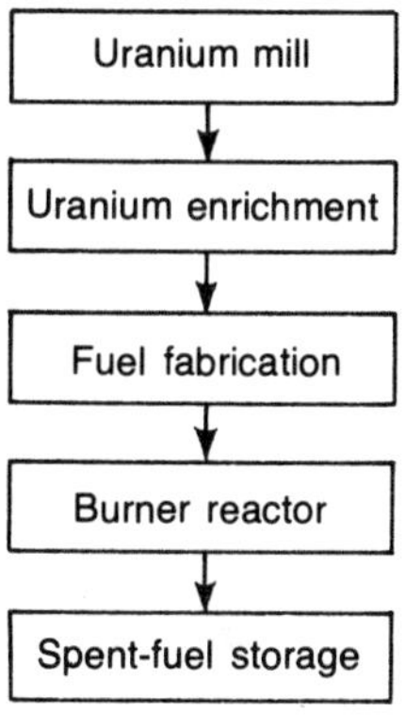

Second, the plutonium contained in the spent fuel from these reactors is mixed with highly radioactive fission products that offer a very effective degree of self-protection against theft. A typical spent-fuel assembly weighs roughly 1/2 metric ton and contains about 4 kilograms of distributed plutonium oxide mixed with fission products and uranium oxide. Two months after removal from the reactor, this material would deliver in a few seconds a lethal dose of gamma radiation to a person standing next to it without shielding. After removal from a reactor during refueling operations, spent-fuel assemblies are stored for several months or more in large water pools that provide both cooling and shielding. Removing the several fuel assemblies required to contain enough plutonium for a crude fission bomb would require the use of heavy cranes, at least several tons of shielded containers to protect thieves from the radiation after removal from the water, and a large truck to transport the shielded, stolen fuel assemblies. Containers now used for shipping spent fuel to another storage pool weigh more than 20 tons, and containers used for rail shipment weigh as much as 100 tons. Even if thieves managed somehow to steal spent-fuel assemblies, they would be faced with an extremely dangerous and technically difficult job of extracting the plutonium in a concentrated form suitable for nuclear explosives. The obstacles to small groups interested in acquiring the materials for a plutonium-type bomb from a once-through system are not as insurmountable as for enriching uranium but are formidable nonetheless.

Thus with modest physical security precautions, the present type of once-through fuel cycle that characterizes most of the world's nuclear power systems can be very effectively safeguarded against theft and subsequent use in nuclear explosives by criminal groups, even if they possess skills, resources, and determination considerably beyond those historically displayed in professional thefts of valuables.

But the once-through cycle fails to make use of the full power-generation potential of nuclear material. The plutonium in the spent fuel is not *inextricably* mixed with the fission products and can be put to further use as reactor fuel. Its chemical removal from spent fuel forms the foundation of the plutonium economy, the recycle of plutonium in light-water reactors and in breeders (depicted in Figure 2). Such an eventuality will drastically undermine the intrinsic safeguards of the once-through fuel cycle. For recycling plutonium will require its separa-

FIGURE 2

Projected Plutonium Breeder Fuel Cycle

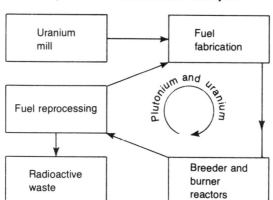

tion, fabrication, stockpile, and transport in forms far more accessible to criminal groups than if the spent fuel is simply disposed of. It will introduce weapons-grade material into a central position in the civilian nuclear power fuel cycle.

The quantity of weapons-grade material that will have to be safeguarded under full-scale plutonium recycle is striking. For example, Table 1 shows the amounts of plutonium to be produced annually in about 30 countries in 1983 if their present plans for nuclear power development are fulfilled. The world sum, as noted, will be more than 75,000 kilograms annually. (The mass of plutonium needed to make a crude nuclear explosive is in the range of 5 to 20 kilograms.) The cumulative quantity of plutonium produced during the next decade and a half we estimate at over 2 million kilograms. In addition to these staggering quantities of material to be protected in the normal course of commercial power operation, we may suppose also that in a plutonium recycle economy there would be a substantial number of research facilities employing and working with weapons-grade material.

In the face of this safeguards challenge, it is noteworthy that even the industrialized countries closest to the introduction of a plutonium economy have not yet displayed clearly how they intend to manage and secure the plutonium that will soon be available. The character and scope of the threats that the security systems should be designed to cope with, the extent to which military and paramilitary security forces

141

TABLE 1
Installed Nuclear Power and Plutonium Production by Country, ca 1983

Country	Projected Total Nuclear Generating Capacity Installed, Under Construction, and Planned (MWe)	Annual Net Plutonium Production Rate at Projected Nuclear Capacity (kg/yr)
Argentina	920	340
Austria	690	160
Belgium	1,660	380
Brazil	3,200	1,000
Bulgaria	1,760	410
Canada	11,800	4,400
Czechoslovakia	1,870	430
Finland	2,160	500
France	15,700	3,900
Germany (Dem. Rep.)	2,700	620
Germany (Fed. Rep.)	22,500	5,200
Hungary	1,760	410
India	1,680	490
Iran	4,200	970
Italy	5,300	1,200
Japan	15,500	3,600
Luxembourg	1,300	300
Mexico	1,320	300
Netherlands	530	120
Pakistan	125	45
Philippines	1,250	290
Poland	440	100
Rumania	440	100
South Korea	1,800	500
Spain	9,200	2,100
Sweden	8,350	1,900

TABLE 1
Installed Nuclear Power and Plutonium Production by Country,
ca 1983 (Cont.)

Country	Projected Total Nuclear Generating Capacity Installed, Under Construction, and Planned (MWe)	Annual Net Plutonium Production Rate at Projected Nuclear Capacity (kg/yr)
Switzerland	5,900	1,350
Taiwan	5,800	1,350
United Kingdom	11,800	3,300
U.S.*	154,000	35,500
U.S.S.R.	14,000	3,300
Yugoslavia	615	140
Totals	310,000	76,700

*Excludes capacity planned, as of January 1, 1976, after 1983.

SOURCE: *Nuclear Buyers Guide,* mid-February 1976, and T. B. Taylor, "Nuclear Safeguards," *Annual Review of Nuclear Science,* vol. 25, 1975, p. 416.

should be deployed, and the character of the physical security systems to meet the postulated threats are all matters still in dispute in the United States and elsewhere. The outcome of these disputes and the protective systems that will eventually be emplaced in each country are likely to be left almost entirely to the discretion of the individual countries.

International safeguards as now structured permit commerce in weapons-grade material to proceed unencumbered by physical security arrangements other than those imposed by individual nations. There are no existing measures that translate the international community's clear interest in every nation's physical security system into concrete international arrangements. The haphazard drift of the nuclear industry worldwide will soon create, in a large number of countries, fuel cycles dealing with weapons-grade material and guarded with an intensity determined by each individual country alone. Even if, as may be argued, most countries in principle have the technical ability effectively to

143

safeguard plutonium and other weapons-grade material, the institutional and political problems of ensuring that each country dealing with weapons-grade material actually achieves such safeguards appear to us immense. Nearly 50 countries will be handling weapons-grade plutonium, not mixed with fission products, within the next two decades if plutonium is generally recycled in present-type (*not* breeder) reactors during that period.

NATIONAL DIVERSION: THE PROBLEM OF PROLIFERATION

The factors that shape and to a degree lessen the safeguards task of guarding against diversion of weapons-grade material by subnational criminal groups are largely irrelevant to the problem of national diversion. The (presumed) inability of such groups to undertake uranium isotope separation or spent-fuel reprocessing or to construct their own plutonium production reactors cannot be assumed to apply to all nations that might want to acquire nuclear weapons in the future; nor is there any practical international analogue to the security forces that nations can deploy to protect against theft by criminal groups. As a consequence, the safeguards objectives applicable to national proliferation must clearly be different from those directed against criminals and terrorists. Whereas the latter must be simply to prevent physically the acquisition by such groups of weapons-grade material, the former must perforce be more complex, subtle, and modest.

To understand what these objectives might be, consider the ways in which a nation could try to accumulate material for nuclear weapons. Excluding the possibility of direct acquisition of weapons from other countries, there are two fundamental routes open to nations. They can directly undertake a program, quite outside the civilian power sector, to produce weapons-grade material, or they can divert weapons-grade material from their civilian nuclear power programs, clandestinely or openly.

The direct route itself has two paths: the extraction of plutonium or ^{233}U from a reactor and reprocessing plant built to produce weapons material or the enrichment of uranium to weapons-grade concentrations. The first path is already within the capability of a large number of

144

countries. One author estimates, for example, that even quite small and poor countries could build small reactors capable of producing 10 kilograms of plutonium per year at a cost per reactor of tens of millions of dollars or less and with material and design information readily and openly available.[8] A natural uranium, graphite-moderated, air-cooled reactor similar to the Brookhaven graphite research reactor that operated at Brookhaven National Laboratory for a decade appears an especially apt example of the kind of production reactor accessible to small countries. Such a reactor could probably be constructed in less than five years.

In larger or richer countries, especially those with the experience of civilian nuclear power programs, plutonium production reactors could probably be constructed at perhaps one-tenth the cost of a normal power reactor of comparable size. Indeed, on purely economic and technical grounds, it is likely that in most of these countries, construction of separate production reactors would be the preferred route to nuclear weapons, compared with diversion from civilian power programs. The latter would typically require costly interference with normal operating procedures. Production reactors can also be operated to produce plutonium of optimal isotopic composition for weapons (high in ^{239}Pu, low in other plutonium isotopes), whereas commercial reactors, especially the light-water types, cannot be so optimized without their commercial operation being altered significantly. The materials necessary for the operation of a production reactor, with the possible exception of natural uranium, are likely to be available on the open market; but uranium is also very widely distributed, at least in small quantities, among many countries.

The chemical reprocessing technology required to separate the plutonium from irradiated nuclear fuel is, as is the reactor technology, widely available. A commercially competitive nuclear fuel reprocessing plant that produces separated plutonium and uranium that meet the stringent quality control specifications required by the nuclear industry is a highly complex, sophisticated, several-hundred-million-dollar enterprise. But a reprocessing facility designed to extract plutonium only

[8]J. R. Lamarsh, *On the Construction of Plutonium-Producing Reactors by Small and/or Developing Nations,* report to the Library of Congress, Congressional Reference Service, April 30, 1976.

for nuclear weapons could be considerably smaller, simpler, and less expensive. It is indeed possible to describe such a facility in a form that would require only a few months for construction and an operating crew of less than a dozen appropriately skilled people using information that is widely published and materials and equipment that are commercially available on the open market. It is possible for such a facility to be constructed and even operated clandestinely.

The time required to extract plutonium employing the direct route will, of course, vary with the sophistication of the country involved. Most industrialized countries could probably begin to produce and extract substantial amounts of plutonium within 3 years or so of a decision to start the enterprise. Most of the less developed countries would take longer than this, possibly 5 years for a very small program designed to produce several bombs per year up to 8 or 10 years for a somewhat more substantial program.

The direct path to nuclear weapons via uranium enrichment also appears open to several countries. The currently developed technology most suited to such an endeavor appears to be that employing gas centrifuges, although other processes also appear to be practical alternatives. Rathjens and Carnesale, for example, estimate that a gas centrifuge plant adequate to meet the needs of a small weapons program could probably be built by any of several non-nuclear powers at a cost of tens of millions of dollars.[9] The production of weapons-grade uranium could conceivably become still less expensive and less difficult if the current promise of enrichment by the use of lasers is actually fulfilled; as instance of this promise, it has recently been suggested by scientists at Los Alamos National Laboratory and at Exxon Nuclear that laser enrichment looks possible at a cost and energy expenditure a fraction of that required for centrifuges. Whatever process is used, the time required to build and operate an enrichment facility capable of producing significant amounts of weapons-grade uranium would probably be several years for most non-nuclear countries not already deeply involved with enrichment technology.

The second fundamental way a nation may try to obtain weapons-grade material is through its civilian nuclear power program. One way it can do this is by the clandestine diversion of a small fraction of

[9]George Rathjens and Albert Carnesale, private communication, 1975.

weapons-grade material passing through the fuel cycle. Such gradual and secret accumulation of weapons-grade material may look attractive to countries not subject to international or bilateral safeguards agreements (for example, Israel or South Africa), but it is a process that generally appears less politically plausible if the clandestine diversion involves violation of such agreements. The prospect of clandestine diversion would always be cause for concern among adversaries and provides, we believe, one persuasive rationale for the establishment of a strong international safeguards system capable of *detecting* any significant diversion.

Far more likely than clandestine diversion, we believe, is the prospect that a government may simply appropriate a part of its own civilian power program and convert it to weapons material production. The costs and advantages of such drastic action would depend strongly both on the legal safeguard obligations the country had assumed and on the character of the civil program. Certainly the political costs would be highest in those instances in which international and bilateral safeguards arrangements were most clearly violated. But the character of the power program would perhaps be even more important to a government's assessment of risk and gain. In a once-through fuel cycle where there exists no national reprocessing, a country would face a considerable delay between diversion of spent fuel and production of separated plutonium in a reprocessing facility built from scratch. In this case, the direct route to weapons may seem almost as (or more) attractive. Conversely, with plutonium recycle, nations will be able rapidly to turn seized material into weapons manufacture. Most tempting from this perspective would be inadequately guarded stockpiles of separated plutonium.

These various details and uncertainties cannot mask the stark reality—that if a country is determined to acquire nuclear weapons, there are no conceivable technical controls on present or planned nuclear power programs which can prevent it from doing so, either directly or through its civilian program.

Far from suggesting that any controls are therefore useless, however, we strongly argue the contrary, that controls and safeguards could significantly increase the time and the technical and political costs a country would have to expend to acquire nuclear weapons. In this manner, they could substantially affect the resolve of a country to

147

embark on a weapons program. The issue is not whether safeguards alone can stop a determined country from acquiring weapons, but rather whether they can significantly influence that initial determination.

This leads us to consider situations, short of actual diversion of nuclear materials from civilian nuclear facilities, that could relate to a country's decision to acquire nuclear weapons.

LATENT PROLIFERATION

We define latent proliferation to be a situation in which a country, whether deliberately or not, has moved substantially closer to having nuclear weapons than it would be if it had no nuclear programs whatever. Strictly speaking, any nation that has people trained in any aspect of nuclear technology or research, even if it has no nuclear facilities per se, has started to move into this situation, whatever may be the country's long-range intentions. At the other end of the continuum of possible states of latent proliferation is a country that has designed and tested all the required non-nuclear components of several kinds of nuclear weapons, has the military delivery systems for effective use of those weapons, and also has fabricated the necessary nuclear weapon materials into forms such that their insertion into the weapons will immediately give the country a full-fledged nuclear arsenal. And there is a practically infinite number of conceivable states in between.

We address this subject in some detail here because we believe it has so far received far less international attention than it deserves. Until fairly recently, perhaps until the time of the Indian nuclear detonation, most people concerned with nuclear proliferation seemed to suggest that a country's progress toward acquiring nuclear weapons would always proceed through a *sequential* set of steps—from a reactor or an enrichment facility to a reprocessing plant (if required), to the design of a weapon, to fabrication and test of non-nuclear components of weapons, to a transfer of some nuclear weapons material, to a test weapon, to a nuclear test, at which point proliferation would be considered complete. When considering safeguards against further proliferation that makes use of civilian nuclear power facilities, people have generally seen the crucial step as the transfer of the plutonium or other weapons-grade material out of a civilian facility to a weapons fabrication facility. It is this act that international and most bilateral nuclear safeguards are designed to detect and, by the threat of political repercussions, deter.

But as we try to show here, many situations that can have severe international security implications are much more complex and difficult to deal with than the relatively well-defined act of transferring nuclear materials from where they are authorized to be to where they are not. We can illustrate this problem by the following far from complete list of examples of various conceivable states of latent proliferation:

- A "non-nuclear-weapons state" that either has uranium enrichment facilities or one or more reactors and a small reprocessing facility has secretly designed and tested the non-nuclear components of fission weapons and a small plant for fabricating nuclear weapon cores, has a stockpile of nuclear weapons without nuclear cores, and has military systems for their effective delivery. We find it credible that several such states of latent proliferation could exist today. We should also point out that as far as we know, the *first* tests of all nuclear explosives by all nations, using either enriched uranium or plutonium, have been successful, suggesting that a high degree of dependability can be assumed even in the absence of a test detonation.

- A country that has no major nuclear power facilities but does have a significant nuclear research program and is constructing one or more power reactors is secretly designing nuclear explosives and the facilities required to extract plutonium from the forthcoming reactors, to have the option of using it in nuclear weapons. We find it highly credible that several such situations could exist now.

- A nation, whether or not it now has any major nuclear facilities, now knows in detail what it would do if it decided to build nuclear weapons. This is now a possibility in any country that has the appropriately skilled technical people.

- A non-nuclear-weapons state that has a commercial reprocessing plant has a stockpile of several thousand kilograms of purified plutonium oxide, has not actually built any nuclear weapons fabrication facilities, but is generally aware of what it would need to do to incorporate the plutonium into nuclear weapons. We find this to be a highly likely state in any country with a commercial reprocessing plant.

It is expected that many countries will in the long run wish to narrow the time and cost of converting at least parts of their civilian programs to weapons production. They will wish to keep their options open so as to be able to initiate steps toward the unconditional acquisition of weapons-grade material without clearly being perceived as having done so. In this manner, we may expect countries gradually to constrict the twilight period between decision and weapon, a process that we believe will hasten a nuclear weapons decision. In general, we would expect a government to be far less likely to launch a weapons program that could not reach fruition until well after the expected life of the government itself than to do so when the critical material was already at hand and much of the necessary resources already expended. A country with large plutonium stockpiles would be more likely to stumble or to be driven into a nuclear weapons decision than one without such stockpiles. We think it would also discourage proliferation if countries were not in a position to acquire nuclear weapons quickly in response to some external event (such as, let us say, the Indian nuclear explosion in 1974) and before there was time for the international community to marshal a collective response.

There is, in principle, much that can happen to narrow drastically the twilight period between decision and weapon. Developments such as plutonium recycle, for example, can sharply foreshorten the time needed to extract weapons-grade material and badly obfuscate distinctions between civilian power and weapons activities. It appears to us that a salient objective of safeguards should be to prevent, to the extent possible, such latent proliferation, by imposing as sharp and vivid a distinction as practical between activities intrinsic to a nation's civilian nuclear power program and those required for the acquisition of weapons. Such a safeguards objective is to be sought in the controls applied to civilian power programs. If safeguards on nuclear power are haphazard, lax, and without explicit international prohibitions on certain classes of activity (such as, for example, reprocessing and plutonium recycle), countries will increasingly be in a position to obfuscate their intentions and to prepare themselves technically to move rapidly along one of the direct paths to nuclear weapons.

The latent proliferation that a safeguard strategy should be designed to counter is already under way. The first manifestation of latent proliferation is the development in several non-nuclear countries of an independent fuel cycle and the technical competence that will permit them with increasing technical ease (disregarding legal constraints) to obtain weapons-grade material. The spread of nuclear reactors is the earliest stage in the development and is of course already well established, as noted in Table 1.

At present, India is the only less developed country with an indigenous capability to manufacture its own reactor and reactor components. But we may expect this situation to change in the next decade as more countries that must now import nuclear technology gradually accumulate sufficient experience, material, and knowledge to go out on their own. We should also expect a growing number of countries gradually to become practically independent of foreign sources of fuel supply. The few countries now constructing CANDU reactors will need only natural uranium, a commodity now widely available all over the world in small amounts. Although the larger number of countries deploying light-water reactors will have to depend on some source of uranium enrichment as well as on natural uranium, this technology also promises to become more widespread. South Africa and Brazil, for example, have declared plans for the construction of at least pilot enrichment facilities, the Brazilians albeit with assistance from the West Germans.

Several harbingers of plutonium recycle now promise to advance latent proliferation still another degree. Reprocessing plants are now or soon will be operating in at least six countries: the United Kingdom, France, West Germany, India, Japan, and the Soviet Union. Three of these countries (the United Kingdom, Germany, and France) have joined together to form a multinational reprocessing service, United Reprocessors, with a plant under construction in West Germany. The United States has completed construction of a large reprocessing plant at Barnwell, South Carolina, but the start of operations has been delayed pending regulatory review. In the United States also, the Nuclear Fuel Service plant at West Valley, New York, which operated between 1966 and 1972, might resume operation in the early 1980s, and Exxon Corporation has announced plans for a third large reprocessing plant to be built in the 1980s. With such activity vigorously under way in the most industrialized countries of the West and in Japan, it is to be expected that many other countries are now planning to undertake their own reprocessing. And indeed, Argentina, Brazil, Italy, Pakistan, Spain, and Yugoslavia have already announced plans to build reprocessing plants. In recent negotiations with potential nuclear supplier countries, Iran and Brazil have evidently refused to enter agreements that could prevent them from undertaking their own reprocessing. Iran, evidently with no specific reprocessing plans, nonetheless apparently withdrew, in early 1976, from a prospective multiple-reactor purchase from the United States over American insistence that no spent fuel from the reactors be reprocessed in Iran. With so much reprocessing and freedom to reprocess going forward, it does not appear likely that very many countries will forego the option without new and far-reaching safeguards agreements.

Despite the great interest in reprocessing, no country has yet embarked on the large-scale use of plutonium in commercial reactors. But the momentum is clear. The United Kingdom, France, West Germany, Italy, Japan, the Soviet Union, and the United States all have significant programs of breeder development under way. The French have already constructed a prototype breeder, and another commercial-size prototype is being constructed with financial assistance from W. German and Italian utilities. The West Germans also have a large breeder prototype under construction, and an experimental breeder of French design is now being built in the south of India. Without significant new governmental initiatives, it appears likely that in another 10 years or so, several countries will be engaged in substantial recycle of plutonium, with plutonium becoming a staple of nuclear commerce, routinely separated, fabricated, traded, and stockpiled. Such at least is the vision of several countries.

Coupled with these technical aspects of latent proliferation are various weaknesses in the current framework of international safeguards which could increasingly unshackle countries from legal constraints on the disposal of their civilian nuclear power programs. This safeguards framework is dominated juridically by the Non-Proliferation Treaty (NPT) and technically by the safeguards system of the International Atomic Energy Agency (IAEA). With respect to the NPT, difficulties derive both from countries that have refused to join the Treaty and from those that have joined. The nonparties (including Brazil, Argentina, India, Pakistan, Egypt, Israel, South Africa, and Spain) remain free to construct unsafeguarded facilities, whether or not they are receiving nuclear assistance from abroad. They will thus eventually be able to mimic facilities supplied under safeguards and will be able to produce completely unrestricted weapons-grade material. With respect to countries that are party to the Treaty, there are two sorts of problems, both related to withdrawal from the Treaty. Some of the countries are already in a position to acquire weapons-grade material and develop nuclear weapons without foreign assistance. The safeguards accepted by these countries (West Germany, Japan, Sweden, Canada) on many of their facilities are obligations incurred by a voluntary accession to the NPT and can thus be removed by formal withdrawal from the Treaty, a nontrivial political act but an available legal option nonetheless. Even plutonium stockpiles produced before withdrawal would presumably be freed from any safeguards restrictions once withdrawal was effected. A similar vulnerability exists for parties to the Treaty that do not have strong indigenous technology. These countries (including, for example, Libya and South Korea) would appear, under Article IV of the NPT, to have a strong argument that they should receive whatever legitimate nuclear assistance they wish so long as the assistance and the attached safeguards conditions are consistent with the NPT. The danger is again that the countries may eventually formally withdraw from the Treaty and consequently from their NPT obligations as well. Facilities previously exported to other countries by the United States (and Canada) under the NPT would revert to coverage under bilateral safeguards after withdrawal, an important insurance. However, in the case of other supplier countries, the status of safeguards after a recipient withdraws from the NPT is unclear; and it is evident that any facilities developed indigenously by a country will, under present conditions, be safeguard-free after withdrawal.

Vulnerabilities that can give further impulse to latent proliferation appear also in the IAEA safeguards system, since lack of trust in the reliability of established safeguards may cause states to hedge against proliferation by themselves moving closer to a weapons capability. The IAEA has the responsibility for imposing safeguards to detect diversion of nuclear materials from peaceful to unauthorized purposes by countries that are parties to the NPT or that have otherwise agreed to place their civilian nuclear materials under international safeguards. The safeguards system adopted by the IAEA to perform this function is based primarily on materials accounting procedures and, to an increasing extent, on inspection, tamper-proof surveillance, and seal techniques designed to detect unauthorized operations. There is concern that the personnel and resources available to the IAEA to undertake these responsibilities are inadequate and that the Agency's concern to nourish nuclear power around the world will also sap its safeguards vigilance.

In addition, its resource limitations have forced the IAEA to rely

153

substantially on national systems of inspection, in which the principal IAEA function is to test statistically national materials accounts. The emphasis is on statistical techniques and strategic points measurements rather than on human or instrument surveillance and independent materials balance measurements by the IAEA. The safeguards system thus depends significantly on the cooperation of the country being inspected. At the same time, the inspection procedures actually implemented in a country are considered *safeguards-confidential,* i.e., all safeguards information—except that pertaining to a few members of the IAEA inspectorate—is classified outside the country. No country can know if the safeguards procedures it accepts are harsher than those for its neighbor; the international community cannot know how effective are the safeguards procedures actually applied.

These vulnerabilities will not sow their consequences immediately. In general, unless the critical non-nuclear weapons countries are willing to break bilateral agreements with the United States and Canada, they cannot acquire weapons-grade material legally usable for weapons before the mid-1980s. The agreements now being forged between France and Germany and countries such as Brazil, Pakistan, and Iran will also not reach fruition until such time at the earliest.

The crucial thresholds toward independent access to weapons-grade material are thus not likely to take place for another 5 to 10 years if the states that export nuclear technology, the United States above all, maintain a strong insistence on the continued adherence by the affected countries to their safeguards obligations. The situation could dramatically change by the mid-1980s, however, when several countries will have begun to accumulate a plutonium stockpile (albeit under safeguards). The current situation is thus one marked by a drift past various points of no return where technical and legal barriers to national and criminal diversions of weapons-grade material are one by one eroded.

THREE

Principles for Effective Safeguards

In the face of this drift and of the present inadequacies of national and international safeguards, we believe that the world should establish, with a sense of utmost urgency, as effective as practicable safeguards against both criminal and national diversion. The objectives of such a system have been implicitly derived in the preceding section; they can, we believe, be usefully formulated as a set of guiding principles. The first two principles focus on the problem of criminal diversions, the final three on the problem of nuclear proliferation.

1. *All weapons-grade material, whether at fixed sites or in transport, should be effectively protected against criminal theft or diversion through the use of techniques that are open to inspection and assessment by all interested nations.*

    International safeguards as now structured permit commerce in weapons-grade material unencumbered by physical security arrangements other than those imposed by individual nations. There are no existing measures that translate the international community's clear interest in every nation's physical security system into concrete international arrangements. This principle insists, by contrast, that national systems of physical security over weapons-grade material should be monitored by the international community. Thus not only would states have to meet minimal international standards, but they also could be relatively confident that other states were also conforming.

2. *Internationally managed physical security safeguards, nevertheless, should not be required at national facilities.*

This principle recognizes the generally strong resistance of countries to any actions that suggest infringement of national sovereignty over internal law enforcement. Since reactors are by far the most numerous of nuclear facilities as well as the fuel-cycle component that countries are most reluctant to site outside of their boundaries, the principle implies that reactors should be designed to minimize the problem of physical security at and en route to reactor sites.

3. *All nuclear materials for civilian use, and from which weapons-grade materials can be derived, should be kept within authorized channels defined by specific physical boundaries, and any transfers of strategic quantities of these materials outside these boundaries must be promptly detected by an IAEA or equivalent international safeguards system.*

This principle reflects the essential objective of the current international safeguards system. This system can at best hope to detect diversions of material; it is not designed, nor can it expect, to prevent diversions.

The physical boundaries need not necessarily be stationary. They might include, for example, the containers or vehicles used for transportation of safeguarded nuclear materials. For the present, we define "strategic quantities" to be such that the contained quantities of ^{235}U, plutonium, or ^{233}U be more than 5 kilograms, 1 kilogram, and 1 kilogram, respectively. By "promptly" we mean essentially at the time any unauthorized movement out of authorized channels takes place. This implies that emphasis would be placed by the IAEA on direct surveillance by instruments or inspectors of credible points at which such transfers might take place and that materials accounting procedures would be used to *supplement* the prompt detection techniques.

Instruments now exist that under some conditions could, in a few seconds or less, detect as little as a few grams of weapons-grade material moving through a doorway or other penetration of a physical boundary. In some situations, accurate materials accounting systems could also detect diversions of less than strategic quantities of nuclear materials. We therefore argue that any detected, unauthorized transfers of *less* than strategic quantities also be recorded by the

156

IAEA and if analyses of these quantities over time indicate that more than a strategic quantity has been diverted from a particular facility, that this be reported by the IAEA inspectorate to the Agency's Board of Governors.

4. *The activities intrinsic to civilian nuclear programs within a country should be as distinct as possible from activities that the country would have to undertake to produce nuclear weapons.*

   This principle emerges from considerations of latent proliferation, that is the tendency of some types of civilian nuclear power programs automatically to lessen the time and technical effort required for the actual production of nuclear weapons.

5. *All safeguards measures and restrictions on access to specific civilian nuclear technologies should be equitably applied to all countries.*

   We believe it illusory to suppose that a safeguards system can long persist that formally denies some aspects of *civilian* nuclear technology to certain countries while permitting them to others and that otherwise imposes safeguards obligations discriminately. Beyond the asymmetric safeguards obligations that now exist under the Non-Proliferation Treaty between the nuclear weapon states and the non-nuclear states, there are increasing international efforts to discriminate between classes of non-nuclear countries. Several of the industrialized countries with the strongest indigenous programs of civilian nuclear power hope to deny technologies that they themselves plan to develop (such as reprocessing plants) to as many other countries as possible. Still more discriminatorily, several of these nuclear suppliers have sometimes sought or have felt obliged by prior commitments to make distinctions on a country-by-country basis. The United States and other suppliers are prepared to provide nuclear assistance to India and South Africa, which are nonsignatories of the NPT, but are not willing to do so to some countries that are parties to the Treaty. These distinctions are not necessarily unreasonable as a short-term expedient, but they do not form a basis for an enduring, stable policy. They will eventually seem unfair and unpersuasive to supplier countries as well as to the countries denied assistance.

   There is, of course, a deep inequity intrinsic to any nonproliferation strategy, between the countries that have nuclear weapons and the countries that are to be denied them; and in the long run, we doubt that any strategy to impede proliferation can succeed without directly confronting the nuclear weapons already in existence. We do believe, however, that schemes of control on civilian nuclear power that build an international equity into at least this limited sector and that construct a significant reliance on international institutions will provide useful bridges to the more far-reaching international arrangements affecting nuclear weapons that will eventually be necessary.

FOUR

Three Alternative Fission Futures

We shall now examine the compatibility of the preceding guiding principles for safeguards with three fundamentally different fission futures:

1. A *phase-out,* in which nuclear fission power worldwide grows very slowly or not at all in the short term and then eventually is replaced by alternative, nonfission sources of energy, before high-quality uranium resources are used up and without any recycle of weapons-grade material.

2. A *plutonium economy,* in which the worldwide nuclear industry is increasingly dominated by the recycle of plutonium in light-water reactors and eventually by the national deployment of plutonium fast breeder reactors.

3. An *international thorium fuel cycle,* in which much of the nuclear fuel cycle is under international control, with the exception of the reactors, and where the essential breeding cycle is thorium-^{233}U.

PHASE-OUT OF FISSION POWER

The overwhelming majority of nuclear power plants in operation, under construction and on order (light-water and heavy-water reactors) do not employ weapons-grade material as fuel but do produce plutonium. Safeguards against diversion therefore depend above all on what is done

NUCLEAR PROLIFERATION

with the plutonium in the spent fuel. Even a freeze and eventual phase-out of nuclear power will not immediately diminish the severity of this plutonium disposal problem. A 1977 freeze on all new construction starts would still lead to an annual worldwide plutonium production in 1980 of 30,000 kilograms, in 1990 of 90,000 kilograms, and cumulative production of plutonium between now and 1990 of about ½ million kilograms.

There are several possibilities for the disposal of the reactor spent fuel, some of which involve the prior separation of the contained plutonium and some not. However, in the context of a planned phase-out of nuclear power, in which the use of recycled plutonium is rendered unnecessary, a safeguards strategy compatible with our principles can most practically be founded on a simple international convention that spent fuel not be reprocessed anywhere for plutonium recovery, except possibly at a few international centers under international control. The spent fuel could be disposed of at a few sites, preferably in the nuclear weapons states, and under IAEA safeguards. Such a scheme has an attractive simplicity. It denies to nations plutonium in the form in which it could be used for weapons, and it establishes a fuel cycle within each nation in which the opportunity for illicit diversion of weapons-grade material by subnational groups is minimized. Restrictions would apply equally to nuclear weapons states and non-nuclear-weapons states. In such circumstances, all of our safeguards principles could be satisfied.

Quite apart from any intention to use plutonium in recycle or in bombs, there may be good reasons to remove the plutonium and other long-lived isotopes—*actinides*—from spent fuel prior to disposal. Such a procedure would separate the more lastingly dangerous radioactive isotopes from the bulk of the high-level wastes and thereby potentially simplify the disposal of these wastes. However, the low-level wastes produced by the actinide separation may turn out to be sufficiently troublesome to more than offset any resultant simplification of the high-level waste problem. If, in the long run, separation before disposal is called for, we believe it could be accomplished at a very few sites under international control, and thus in a manner consistent with our safeguards principles. Plutonium thus produced could then either be disposed of or conceivably burned as a fuel at the international facility.

In this connection, we should mention a possible alternative for

160

dealing with spent fuel from light-water reactors recently proposed and under study by the U.S. Arms Control and Disarmament Agency.[10] The idea is to transfer spent, light-water reactor fuel to heavy-water reactors of the CANDU type, to consume further the contained plutonium, ^{235}U, and some of the more troublesome fission products and actinide wastes before ultimate disposal of the fuel. At the time of this writing, the technical, economic, safety, and environmental aspects of this proposal had not yet been examined in any detail. If further analysis should show that this is a viable option, it could be implemented without clashing with any of our guiding principles for safeguards.

It may be, of course, that there is too much reprocessing activity already under way to permit any universal prohibition. But we are not convinced that this is so. The various current and planned activities are in expectation of plutonium recycle and breeders. Were such expectations reversed, the varied national (and multinational) reprocessing activities would mostly be superfluous. There is an important distinction between a once-through system muddling along and a planned commitment to a once-through system for as long as practical, with explicit conventions against recycle. In the former case, there will always be harbingers of recycle, countries planning or half-planning to obtain plutonium for recycle, sale, or storage; clear agreements to safeguard the plutonium effectively will be much more difficult to achieve than if a plan were established to rationalize a once-through system.

On balance, we believe that a once-through system evolving into a planned phase-out of fission power could be effectively safeguarded with an international will to do so. The question is rather whether such an alternative energy future is in any way plausible. We sketch in Chapter Five our reasons for believing that a long-term future without fission may in fact be possible.

However, if our optimistic assessments of the potential of nonfission alternatives to meet world energy needs before high-grade uranium resources are used up are mistaken, then it is likely that the demand for nuclear power will grow rapidly in the next decades. A once-through fuel cycle could not long persist without using up most high-quality uranium resources, and in the face of high demand there would be a

[10]Thomas D. Davies, private communication, 1976.

strong case for breeding. The breeding options are two: uranium-plutonium or thorium-^{233}U. We look at the security implications of these two possibilities in the next two sections, respectively.

A PLUTONIUM ECONOMY

The safeguards problem becomes markedly more complex and difficult if plutonium is to be separated, fabricated, and recycled. A variety of measures to safeguard plutonium under these conditions have been suggested. They are generally of two types: those that could apply more or less equally to all countries, and those aimed specifically at specific classes of non-nuclear powers. We do not try here to survey these systematically, but rather to suggest why we believe that although, from technical and economic standpoints, they could lead to prompt detection of any significant materials diversion and effectively guard against criminal theft of weapons-grade materials, they could not be implemented worldwide without violating some of our guiding principles.

Generally Applicable Safeguards

With respect to the national diversion problem (the problem of proliferation), the foundation of any practical control scheme would probably have to be the institution of an effective and nearly universal international safeguards system to *detect* diversion of weapons-grade material. From a technical and economic perspective, we believe that such a system can indeed be effectively established. But the political and institutional obstacles are considerable. It does not appear likely to us that an effective international safeguards system can in fact be emplaced simply by a gradual extension of the reach of the NPT and of bilateral and IAEA safeguards. The political factors that have so far impeded the development and deployment of safeguards will, in our view, likely continue to do so unless the general context of international nonproliferation efforts is radically altered in the direction of increased international control over the nuclear fuel cycle.

The idea of this sort which has recently received the most attention is that of a regional (or multinational) facility to provide nations access, on favorable terms, to a critical fuel-cycle component—notably, enrichment, reprocessing, waste disposal, and/or fabrication—thereby discouraging national control over the component. One can also imagine a regional service to provide transportation of nuclear material under safeguards. The regional idea is certainly practical from a cold commercial viewpoint. There are now believed to be economies of scale with respect to enrichment and reprocessing which give advantage to large-scale units capable of serving the reactor operations of several countries. Despite such economic advantages, most states will probably not find the economic arguments for regionalization alone compelling. This is particularly so for reprocessing. Although they might not be efficient, relatively small reprocessing plants can certainly be built at a fraction of the cost of a single reactor. It seems unlikely that reprocessing costs should ever exeed 5 percent of the total costs of producing power, a significant figure for a mature commercial nuclear industry in the developed countries, but not a large one when compared with the costs of the energy independence sought by most countries. The more powerful arguments for regionalization will rather be political and institutional—the opportunity for a nation to develop its nuclear industry without concern about reprocessing, radioactive waste management, waste disposal, safeguards, etc.

Despite these real advantages, there may be adduced in several countries at least two arguments against reliance on regional facilities. First, regionalization would seem to place a country's energy security in the control of others and provide a hostage to its own political flexibility quite aside from the question of nuclear weapons. South Africa, for example, probably would not place much trust in a multinational group, all the more so were the group regionally organized. Second, many countries would no doubt be reluctant to share technology with regional competitors whom they do not fully trust. Brazil and Argentina may be cases in point here; or India and Pakistan; or Israel, Egypt, and Iran.

Even were the countries to agree to participate in regional facilities, the consequences for nonproliferation might not all be favorable. First, there is a danger that regional facilities would quicken the spread of certain complex technology. This would appear to be a particular risk for enrichment technology. Second, regional centers—for example, reprocessing plants—could encourage (and subsidize) the expansion of nuclear power and, conceivably, the adoption of plutonium recycle and breeder technology in the less developed countries (LDCs) well before such developments would otherwise appear economically and politically attractive. Third, nations would presumably remain free to construct small and effective (albeit commercially inefficient) reprocessing plants relatively quickly. Since the spent fuel from national reactors would still contain large quantities of plutonium, the existence of regional facilities would not foreclose the possibility of national recovery of plutonium. Fourth, regionalization of recycled plutonium fuel fabrication plants would lengthen transportation links for fresh fuel (which would contain weapons-grade material), perhaps even through countries not parties to the regional reprocessing agreements. This would *increase* the risks of theft of weapons materials en route back to national power plants.

The central difficulty in imposing international or multinational fuel service facilities upon a mature plutonium economy dominated by national fast breeder reactors is that countries would still need to handle and to stockpile large quantities of plutonium usable for weapons. For this reason, even the establishment of wide international participation in multinational centers would not lead to the achievement of our fourth safeguards principle: that civilian and weapons programs be sharply distinct. To do so would require not only a proscription of national reprocessing and uranium enrichment but as well a proscription of national power plants using recycled plutonium, whether or not they are fast breeders. Since in the context of a plutonium economy, this does not appear practical across the board, there has been some thought given to restricting such prohibitions to certain classes of countries, notably the LDCs—that is deviating from our last safeguards principle, respecting equity. This possibility is discussed below in the section on geographically restricted safeguards (pp. 170–173).

With respect to physical security against criminal diversion, a combination of measures to safeguard a plutonium economy may be envisioned. To help design and assess these measures, a concept called the *principle of containment* has been proposed by one of us.[11] According to this principle, all nuclear power industry would be contained in areas circumscribed by a well-defined set of barriers. These barriers would exclude unauthorized persons. A minimum number of authorized chan-

[11]Willrich and Taylor, *Nuclear Theft,* p. 159.

nels for the flow of nuclear materials through the barriers would be established. All other channels would be continuously monitored, by means of the best available technology, to detect any unauthorized flow of materials. Such containment could, for example, be manifested by: (1) physical barriers at fixed sites designed to prevent unauthorized penetration long enough to ensure that on-site or reserve guard forces arrive on the scene before the theft is completed, with the capacity to deal with any credible type of attempted theft; (2) shipment of nuclear materials in massive containers and vehicles designed to resist penetration and transfer of the shipment to another vehicle, and the use of reserve guard forces able to deal with any theft attempt; (3) provision of automatic alarms that would immediately detect attempts to remove materials from authorized channels and sound alarms at several specified control points; and (4) provision of on-site and in-transit guard forces for the purpose of denying access of unauthorized people to places where nuclear materials exist.

The principle of containment could also encompass the establishment of a national nuclear materials accounting system that contained electronically reported, accurate data from all nuclear facilities concerning the quantities, physical and chemical forms, and locations of all safeguarded nuclear materials. Present materials accounting requirements of the U.S. Nuclear Regulatory Commission call for periodic reporting of nuclear material balance accounts and input-output material balance accuracies for special nuclear materials that are between 0.5 and 1 percent, depending on the types of materials and facilities. These uncertainties could amount to several dozen kilograms or more of plutonium per year at a large fuel reprocessing or fuel fabrication plant, enough material for at least several nuclear explosives. One way to improve these accuracies considerably would be to monitor all points of access to a facility that contained special nuclear materials using instruments designed to detect the removal of very small quantities of special nuclear material through channels (such as personnel exits) that are *not* authorized channels for the flow of these materials. For example, instruments that can detect the presence of 1 gram or less of unshielded plutonium, at a distance of a few feet and in about 1 second are commercially available. Use of such devices, along with highly accurate measurements of the flows and inventories of nuclear materials in *authorized* channels, could provide a high level of assurance that not even very small quantities of materials had been surreptitiously removed from nuclear facilities. Any recorded significant changes in the amounts or forms of nuclear materials could be immediately reported by direct communication links to a central, national data storage and processing system.

In some respects, the normal operation of a plutonium recycle economy would facilitate certain of these measures. For example, it is likely that rather massive shielding from gamma rays and, in some cases, neutron radiation would be required to ensure that radiation exposure to workers at all points in the fuel cycle for systems that used recycled plutonium was insignificant. This would mean that for reasons not connected with safeguards, heavy containers and barriers would have to be used in the storage, transport, and fabrication of nuclear fuels from the time they were separated at a reprocessing plant to the time they were placed in reactors for refueling. These barriers and containers would make theft much more difficult. If the plutonium were removed from such barriers, however, the penetrating radiation levels, though higher than industry standards will allow, would not be a significant deterrent to theft, since they would deliver considerably less than disabling or lethal doses to people close by, even after hours of exposure.

In addition to these general measures to secure plutonium in transport and to rationalize physical protection at fixed sites, certain alterations of the fuel cycle itself should be examined for their safeguards effectiveness: in particular, *blending* of plutonium and uranium fuels, *co-location* of principal national nuclear facilities, and spiking and denaturing of nuclear material.

Present plans in the United States and elsewhere where recycle is being considered call for the plutonium to be separated as a nitrate and converted to plutonium oxide at the reprocessing plant. After reprocessing, the material would be shipped to a mixed-oxide fabrication plant where the plutonium oxide was blended with natural uranium oxide to produce mixed-oxide rods. Then the mixed-oxide rods would be shipped to a plant that assembled the mixed-oxide rods with slightly enriched uranium rods (fabricated elsewhere). The concentration of plutonium in the mixed-oxide rods would be about 5 percent; its concentration in the final assembly would be about 2 percent. These planned procedures do not appear ideal from a safeguards perspective, and some of the measures that have been proposed to improve physical security involve different blending arrangements.

One alternative, for example, is to dilute the separated plutonium by slightly enriched or natural uranium at the output stages of reprocessing plants to produce the mixed-oxide fuel materials *before* the plutonium is shipped to a fuel fabrication plant. In equilibrium, the concentration of plutonium in the mixed-oxide fuel would be about 0.6 to 1 percent if all refabricated fuel for a light-water reactor power system consisted of mixed oxide. This would increase by about a factor of 100 the total weight of fuel material that would have to be stolen in order for a given weight of contained plutonium to be obtained. Intermediate blending concentrations, not involving mixing *all* uranium with *all* the plutonium at the reprocessing plant, are also possible.

An alternative at the opposite extreme from this dilution would be the recycle of fuel with as *high* a concentration of plutonium as possible through a *small* fraction of the power plants that produce plutonium, the necessary blending of uranium and plutonium oxide also being performed at the reprocessing plant, before the plutonium is shipped to a fuel fabrication plant. The purpose in doing this would be to reduce to a minimum the number of power plants that receive fuel that contains plutonium as well as the total number of shipments of material with high plutonium content. Under such conditions, all plutonium could be recycled, but fewer than one-half and perhaps as few as about one-fifth of all power plants would use recycled plutonium.

As a complement or alternative to blending, some particularly vulnerable transportation links could be removed if nuclear fuel-cycle facilities were located at the same sites (co-located). Shipments of concentrated plutonium oxide or plutonium nitrate could be avoided if fuel reprocessing facilities and fuel fabrication plants that used their output were next to each other. Facilities for intermediate conversion of plutonium or highly enriched uranium, which are often now located by themselves, could be an integral part of fuel reprocessing or fabrication facilities. As an extreme extension of this concept, *all* fuel-cycle components that handle fissionable materials, including very high capacity power reactors, could be co-located. Doing this would not only remove the need for transportation of fissionable materials over large distances but would also reduce, through economies of scale, the overall costs of safeguards for a complete fuel cycle. It is conceivable that the plutonium economy will, in many countries, ultimately be sited at extremely large centers of this type, to be operated and guarded by paramilitary forces, a drastic but perhaps logical vision of the implications of safeguarding commercial plutonium.

In addition to the blending and co-location schemes to enhance the physical security of weapons-grade materials, measures to modify these materials in such a way as to make them unsuitable for weapons have been suggested. These fall generally into two categories: spiking and denaturing.

Spiking refers generally to the technique of rendering nuclear materials so highly radioactive that they present a mortal danger to those who would attempt to seize them. This result is achieved by the retention of selected fission products in—or the addition of other highly radioactive isotopes, such as ^{60}Co, to—all weapons-grade materials at all stages of nuclear fuel cycles. Extensive studies by the U.S. Nuclear Regulatory Commission (NRC), however, indicate that the concentrations of radioactive "spikants" required to act as serious deterrents to theft would substantially increase fuel-cycle costs. The radioactivity levels required to disable or kill people exposed directly to kilogram quantities of plutonium or highly enriched uranium are more than a million times greater than those that would be unacceptable, without heavy shielding, at all steps in routine fuel fabrication. And the argument that spiking would make theft more difficult by requiring thieves to deal with very heavy shielded containers could also apply for materials that are *not* spiked.

Another alternative similar to spiking, but one that avoids having to deal with intensively radioactive materials during routine fuel fabrication, is to attach large masses of radioactive materials, such as ^{60}Co, to fabricated fuel, to heavily shielded containers for fuel or concentrated plutonium fuel material, or to both fuel and containers. This possibility has also been extensively studied by the NRC and looks technically and economically practical, probably adding less than 1 percent to the overall cost of nuclear electric power.

Use of these safeguards techniques, however, raises a number of legal and safety questions that, as far as we know, have not yet been resolved. It is one thing for the nuclear industry to deal with highly dangerous spent reactor fuel and fission products accumulated at a reprocessing plant. It has to. It is quite another to *add* a serious potential hazard where the technology does not otherwise demand it. One legal question concerning the attached ^{60}Co source scheme relates to the possibility of automatic "summary execution" of people in the act of committing a crime, by means that are explicitly introduced for that purpose. These concerns also apply to the use of spiking substances actually mixed with the fuel materials, if they are deliberately added or retained for the purpose of making them lethal.

Denaturing refers to the addition to weapons-grade materials of a substance that would destroy the suitability of the material for nuclear weapons and that would be very difficult to remove (at least as difficult as isotope separation). Persistent efforts to find such a substance have yielded only one for denaturing ^{235}U or ^{233}U, namely ^{238}U. There is no comparable denaturant for plutonium. This is the critical fact that has focused our attention on the type of thorium cycle explored on pp. 176–183.

From an economic standpoint, all studies we have seen of the direct costs of implementing the kinds of physical security and diversion detection safeguards we have just discussed, as well as others, strongly indicate that the total cost of highly effective safeguards systems would be small, a few percent or less, compared with the total costs of nuclear electric power.

The technical and economic hurdles are high but hardly prohibitive. Rather, it is our concerns about the international political and institutional obstacles to implementation of such safeguards on a worldwide plutonium economy and the persistence of the problem of *latent* proliferation that have led us to believe that it would be extremely difficult, if not impossible, for our guiding principles to be followed in establishing worldwide, effective safeguards for a plutonium economy.

Before summarizing these concerns and our overall conclusions regarding the proliferation aspects of a plutonium economy, we shall briefly discuss some possible, geographically selected restrictions that might assist in controlling plutonium worldwide.

Selected Restrictions

If it appears impractical to effectively safeguard worldwide commercial application of plutonium recycle and breeding, it might be hoped that at least reprocessing and recycling can be restricted to only a few industrialized countries—through agreement if possible or through export impositions if necessary.

The blending scheme mentioned above that seeks to recycle fuel with as high a concentration of plutonium as possible through a small number of reactors provides a possible basis for an agreement to restrict recycle geographically. Reprocessing and recycle would be permitted only in the industrialized countries, and the plutonium produced in the non-recycle countries would be sent to the recycle countries in return for monetary payment or perhaps payment in slightly enriched uranium fuel. Although something like this could perhaps take place for a short period in the normal course of nuclear commerce, we believe it unlikely that it will be possible to maintain a formal two-tier system in the nuclear fuel cycle, keeping certain specific classes of countries plutonium-free more or less indefinitely.

Consider, for example, the kinds of countries one might logically wish to persuade to forego reprocessing, plutonium recycle, and breeders: The LDCs as a whole? All non-nuclear countries? We would expect that the largest of the LDCs—Brazil, Argentina, Mexico, India, South Korea, Taiwan, Iran, and others—would not accept formal restrictions on the deployment of nuclear power not applicable to the developed countries. Nor would a restriction seem feasible that permitted the United States, the Soviet Union, France, the United Kingdom, China, and India to proceed with nuclear power while it was denied to the nonweapons countries—Italy, Germany, Japan, and other powerful countries. Would certain regional clusters of countries be restricted? If, as many observers contend, there is little economic rationale for nuclear power, especially breeders, in most LDCs—even the most advanced, such as India, Brazil, Argentina, and Mexico—a regional renunciation of plutonium recycle in the Middle East, Africa, Latin America, and South and Southeast Asia appears economically (and maybe) politically feasible. However, in Latin America and South and Southeast Asia, vigorous nuclear programs are already under way—in Argentina, Brazil, and Mexico; in India and Pakistan; and in Japan, Taiwan, Korea, and the Philippines. In Africa and the Middle East, where there is not yet the same momentum, some sort of regional contraception of plutonium recycle would be more likely. But in all these regions, whether the ones already committed to nuclear power or the ones not yet so, it seems doubtful that nations will agree to limitations not directed at their "peers" in other parts of the world. Brazil and Argentina, for example, may agree to accept a status different from that of the United States and even from that of the other major nuclear weapon states (although we think not!), but it is hardly believable that they will accept restrictions on their energy options not equally imposed around the world on other non-nuclear states.

If countries would be reluctant to accept formal restrictions on their nuclear programs, perhaps de facto restrictions on plutonium recycle could be imposed by some countries on others through stringent export conditions applied by the few countries now able to produce advanced nuclear equipment. This would, in principle, be done in two somewhat conflicting ways. Exporters could first try to impose legal, technical, and institutional safeguards on the importer's nuclear industry in return for the technology transfer. Or they could simply deny certain material, equipment, and technology to potential importing countries.

Recent and on-going talks among the principal nuclear suppliers (the United States, the United Kingdom, Canada, France, West Germany, Sweden, Japan, and the Soviet Union) have touched on both approaches, although agreement has been achieved only on the first. The suppliers have now agreed on a "trigger list" of export items that will require safeguards, a list that includes essentially all significant nuclear material and equipment. There is now an effort among the suppliers to agree on a common strategy to safeguard transfers of nuclear *technology*, so that receiving countries cannot simply replicate exported equipment in unsafeguarded facilities. However, the suppliers have evidently not been able to agree on the placement of a total export embargo on certain technologies—such as reprocessing plants and isotope separation facilities. Current United States policy is to forbid such transfers, but France and West Germany have recently permitted their nuclear industries to reach agreements with Pakistan and Brazil, respectively, that provide these technologies, at least on a pilot plant basis.

The potential of export agreements to impose safeguards on the international nuclear industry is certainly considerable. Only 11 countries (the United States, the Soviet Union, Canada, France, the United Kingdom, West Germany, Japan, Sweden, Italy, Belgium, and India) can now produce their own nuclear reactors and associated fuel-cycle services. Among the LDCs, only India has an indigenous capacity. The nuclear export industry is even more narrowly based, with but seven companies actually engaged at the moment in the export of

171

nuclear supply systems, the core of a nuclear reactor.[12] Table 2 represents an overview of the industry and the patterns of dependence among the receiver countries. It is evident that agreement among a very few countries could be sufficient to shape the future nuclear industry at least for a while.

Despite this potential export leverage, we are not sanguine that any enduring restriction of plutonium recycle to only a few countries can be imposed simply by export agreement. Already it is clear that the LDCs are vigorously opposed to such an imposition; in the cases of Iran, Pakis-

[12]There are also very few companies now controlling the world market in turbine generators and in other critical assemblies.

TABLE 2
The Nuclear Export Industry

Exporting Country and Company	Importing Country	Operating (MWe)	On Order (Mwe)
Canada (AECL)	Argentina		600
	Pakistan	125	
	India	200	200
	Korea		2 reactors × 600 l.i.†
France (Framatone)	Iran		2 reactors × 900 l.i.
W. Germany (KWU)	Argentina	319	
	Austria		692
	Iran		2 reactors × 1,200 l.i.
	Spain		?
	Switzerland		920
	Netherlands	450	
	Brazil		2 reactors × 1,200 l.i.
Sweden (ASEA/Atom)	Finland		640

†l.i. = letter of intent.

TABLE 2
The Nuclear Export Industry (Cont.)

Exporting Country and Company	Importing Country	Operating (MWe)	On Order (Mwe)
U.S.S.R.	Finland		2 reactors × 420
	Bulgaria	2 reactors × 420	2 reactors × 400
	Czechoslovakia	104	4 reactors × 400
	E. Germany	3 reactors × 400	2 reactors × 440
	Hungary		2 reactors × 440
U.S.A. (GE and Westinghouse)*	Japan		
	Switzerland		
	Sweden		
	India	780	800
	Korea	564	564
	Mexico		2 reactors × 654
	Philippines		2 reactors × 626 l.i.
	Taiwan	604	604
	Spain	3 reactors × 450	4 reactors × 950
		2 reactors × 900	5 reactors × 900
U.S.S.R.	Yugoslavia		615

*Excluding exports to countries that now have indigenous industry and where the United States has no outstanding export orders.

tan, and Brazil at least, the French and West Germans are willing, in part, to respect the LDC point of view. There may eventually be ways to bring suppliers together through such sweeteners as cartel arrangements in which the export market is divided among the principal suppliers or through coercion by the United States involving, for example, a cutoff of enriched uranium to recalcitrant suppliers. If they can, in fact, be achieved, supplier arrangements to forbid the export of reprocessing and other recycle technology may be sensible in the short term;

but unless they are tied to movement toward a future nuclear system in which the safeguards obligations of the industrialized countries and the LDCs are equal, supplier restrictions are sure, we think, to lead eventually to indigenous construction of embargoed facilities by some LDCs which will undermine the suppliers agreements.

Export restrictions are, in our view, a potentially useful means to move toward effective international control of nuclear power, not an alternative to such control. In the context of such movement, the restrictions could form an important part of a transition to any of the alternative futures considered in this paper, especially the phase-out and thorium alternatives.

In sum, we do not think a world split into plutonium users and nonusers can long be sustained. If much of the world embarks upon the plutonium path, one must assume that recycle and breeding will eventually become a worldwide enterprise.

Conclusions Regarding a Worldwide Plutonium Economy

Proceeding from that assumption, is it likely that our guiding principles for safeguarding the plutonium could be effectively carried out? We think not, for the following principal reasons:

The recycle of plutonium in light-water and fast breeder reactors will, as we have noted, force weapons-grade plutonium free of fission products into a central place in the nuclear fuel cycle. Reactors, which for the indefinite future will, in all probability, remain predominantly under national control, will continually be receiving large quantities of this fuel and will require substantial stockpiles of the fresh plutonium at all times in the involved countries. (The plutonium in a fresh fuel load for a fast breeder reactor would typically be about a ton, about four times that for a light-water-reactor plant using recycled plutonium.) Under such conditions, the physical security objectives distilled in the first two principles could be met only with the utmost contrivance and difficulty. Highly effective physical security systems would have to be imposed on the fresh fuel storage facilities at power plants and on all shipments of the fresh fuel to the plants, since the fuel, without contained fission products, is a credible target for theft by criminals. Since inadequacies in this protective system could be the basis of possible criminal or terrorist nuclear threats to other countries, international confidence, presumably including inspection, would be required to assume international security against such threats. We would expect that in a significant fraction of the 50 or so nations that so far have indicated plans to use nuclear power, such inspection and oversight would be considered an unacceptable infringement of national sovereignty. We also note that all of these concerns would exist whether or not fuel were reprocessed at regional fuel-cycle centers and plutonium were shipped back to each country in fresh fuel. Even if, as may be argued, most countries in principle have the technical ability effectively to safeguard plutonium and other weapons-grade material, the institutional and political problems of ensuring that each country dealing with weapons-grade material actually achieves such safeguards appear to us immense. Plutonium recycle does exactly the wrong thing: it focuses the physical security burden at and en route to national reactors.

The potential impact of plutonium recycle on latent proliferation (and therefore on our fourth principle) is especially striking. By involving countries in the separation, fabrication, transport, and stockpiling of weapons-grade material, the plutonium economy would obfuscate irretrievably much of the existing distinction between activities intrinsic to civilian nuclear power production and those required to produce nuclear weapons. Countries would be in a position to move rapidly to nuclear weapons either through the seizure of "civilian" stockpiles of plutonium or through a direct route made easier by a prior construction of "civilian" reprocessing and plutonium fabrication facilities.

These dangers of recycle are apparent and have more or less been recognized by the countries now contemplating reprocessing and recycle. They therefore hope to restrict these activities to only a few industrialized countries. Such an attempt would, of course, contrast sharply with our principle of equity; and although uneven development of new technologies such as recycle may be expected to take place for a short period in the normal course of nuclear commerce, we believe it extremely unlikely that it will be possible to maintain a formal two-tier system in the nuclear fuel cycle so that certain specific classes of countries would be kept plutonium-free indefinitely.

It is primarily for these reasons that we have asked ourselves whether there is a viable alternative to a plutonium economy, based primarily on use of a thorium-^{233}U cycle, that would also allow the fission fuel cycle to be sustained for a very long time without exhausting national fuel sources, as would a once-through system.

175

AN INTERNATIONAL THORIUM CYCLE

As we have seen, a fundamental difficulty with a fission power system based on recycle of plutonium, from a proliferation standpoint, is that weapons-grade plutonium exists in large quantities at all major points of the fuel cycle. There is no way, even in principle, to fix this difficulty by adding a material that will make the plutonium not of weapons grade, as we have defined the term.

^{233}U, the primary fissioning material produced and recycled in the thorium cycle, can, however, be denatured by assuring that wherever it exists it is mixed with enough of the abundant isotope ^{238}U to render it unusable in the core material for a fission explosive unless the ^{238}U has been reseparated. (As noted above, the process of isotope separation is far more difficult than that of chemical reprocessing of plutonium from spent fuel.) This basic fact is the main reason why we strongly urge that possibilities for converting nuclear power systems to the thorium cycle be thoroughly explored.

The critical concentration of ^{233}U in a denatured mixture with ^{238}U, below which it is not possible to sustain a fast chain reaction and therefore make a fission explosive of any kind, is about 4 percent. But even at a concentration as high as 10 to 15 percent and even if the uranium is in pure metallic form, there is a general consensus among experts in nuclear weapon technology that it would not be possible to make a practically usable nuclear explosive. This situation changes rapidly as the ^{233}U concentration in the mixture is increased above 20 percent. Thus above a 30 to 40 percent concentration, the material should definitely be considered to be of weapons grade, though significantly less desirable for weapons than at concentrations above 70 or 80 percent.

Why not keep the concentration of ^{233}U in the denatured mixture below 4 percent, to remove any ambiguity whatever about the suitability of the material for explosives? The reason is that if this were done, roughly as much (or even significantly more) plutonium would be produced from the ^{238}U denaturant by neutron capture as would ^{233}U be produced from thorium. Furthermore, the *conversion ratio* (the ratio of fissionable—that is, reusable—fuel atoms produced to the number consumed) would be so low at 4 percent ^{233}U concentration as to make it impossible to make the entire fuel cycle self-sustaining, in the sense of requiring only ^{238}U or thorium as primary fuel while relying more on the recycle of ^{233}U than on the recycle of plutonium to release most of the energy in the cycle.

Even at a concentration of ^{233}U as high as 15 percent, significant amounts of plutonium would be produced in a reactor using ^{233}U denatured with ^{238}U as fuel. Furthermore, as we discuss in more detail below, the use of *denatured* uranium is certain to degrade the performance of any reactor that would otherwise be using the pure ^{233}U thorium cycle. As far as we know, it is because of this degradation at low concentrations that the use of denatured ^{233}U in thorium-cycle reactors has not been seriously considered until very recently. In general, ^{238}U is something to be avoided in thorium-cycle systems, if attention is given only to reactor performance—to economics and efficient fuel use. The *only* reason we are considering its use to denature ^{233}U for recycling in the thorium fuel cycle is because of our concerns about proliferation and criminal diversion. We think these problems so serious, however, that even substantial degradation in overall fuel cycle performance should be tolerable, as long as some kind of practical overall breeding cycle can be maintained.

Simplified Model of the System at Maturity

In principle at least, one can visualize a thorium-fuel-cycle system that is compatible with *all* of our guiding principles for safeguards.

We first consider how such a system might work in equilibrium, that is, after complete conversion to the new cycle, and at a time when there is no net increase in the number of nuclear power plants in the system. This case is illustrated schematically in Figure 3.

Some number of national power reactors, subject to IAEA safeguards to detect national diversion, are fueled with denatured uranium (e.g., 12 percent ^{233}U and 88 percent ^{238}U) and thorium. Any thorium not actually mixed with the denatured uranium is also mixed with a small amount of ^{238}U, such that the concentration of any ^{233}U produced from the thorium in the reactor will always be less than about 12 percent of the total ^{238}U-^{233}U mixture. The reactors used in this cycle could be converted light-water or heavy-water types or some other suitable type.

Fresh, denatured fuel is shipped to each national power plant from a regional "fuel-cycle support center" at which all spent fuel shipped

FIGURE 3

The Mature Denatured Uranium-Thorium Fuel Cycle

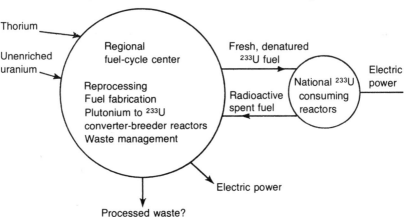

from the national power plants is reprocessed and all fresh, denatured fuel is fabricated. All plutonium contained in the shipments of spent fuel from national reactors is fabricated into fuel for special types of reactors operated only within the regional complex. These special regional reactors have three functions: to consume all plutonium extracted from spent fuel, convert as much of the consumed plutonium as possible to ^{233}U, and produce electric power and/or process heat. All ^{233}U produced in such reactors would then be denatured with ^{238}U and thorium for eventual return to national reactors.

The regional support center would be subject to considerably greater international control than would the outlying national power plants. It would be securely protected from theft, perhaps through the use of a multinational or even international security force. But in any case, the physical security system would be subject to international standards and review procedures. The entire complex would also be subject to IAEA safeguards designed for prompt detection of any unauthorized removal of nuclear materials from the complex.

So far we are presuming that the overall system can be perpetuated by natural supplies of thorium and considerably smaller supplies of natural or depleted uranium provided from some outside source, requiring no isotope enrichment facilities. This is technically supportable but does not in itself ensure the viability of the system.

The key to the technical and economic practicality of the model thorium cycle just described is the way the power produced in the national converter reactors (fueled by the ^{233}U-^{238}U-thorium mix) compares, in equilibrium, with the power produced in the regional breeder reactors (fueled by the plutonium generated in the cycle). If this ratio is high so that the national power plants dominate the power production of the entire system, the role of the regional center will remain an auxiliary one. If, however, the regional breeder reactors produce most of the power in the system, the entire concept will have, in effect, collapsed into a regional "nuclear park." In that case, the technical and economic practicality of the system will depend overwhelmingly on the location of the regional centers—and, of course, on whether or not countries are willing to depend on regional, internationally controlled reactors for most of their nuclear power.

This question turns on the respective capacities of the national and regional reactors to replace fissioned fuel with new fissionable fuel by neutron captures in thorium, to produce ^{233}U, and in ^{238}U, to produce plutonium. A measure of this capacity is called the conversion ratio of a reactor. If it is less than 1 but still appreciable, the reactor is called a *converter* reactor. If it is greater than 1, the reactor is called a *breeder* reactor. The ratio of total power produced by the regional reactors to that produced by all the associated national reactors is directly related to the conversion ratios of the two types of reactors.

If the conversion ratio of the regional reactors is only slightly greater than 1 and the conversion ratio of the national reactors is much less than 1, the overwhelming majority of the useful power produced by the entire system would come from the breeder reactors at the regional center.

If, conversely, the breeding ratio of the regional reactors is high (say, 1.4) and the conversion ratio of the national reactors is close to 1 (say, 0.95), then the power produced by the national reactors could be considerably greater than that produced by the regional reactors (roughly 8 to 1, in this hypothetical case). It is also possible that heavy-water reactors could be designed to achieve conversion ratios equal to or greater than 1, even with denatured uranium.

Unfortunately, this figure of merit for the system depends on a large number of detailed characteristics of reactor design and operating performance which have not yet been systematically studied. It appears that the ratio of national to regional power could be anywhere from very big

179

to very small. In the following section (pp. 180–182) we try to suggest why the situation is so complex. This technical discussion may be safely passed by the lay reader who has already had more than enough exposure to nuclear physics in this paper.

The ratio of ^{238}U to ^{233}U in fresh fuel shipped to the national reactors is approximately 8 to 1 (i.e., the ^{233}U concentration is approximately 12 percent). The ratio of thorium (^{232}Th) to ^{233}U in this fresh fuel might be anywhere in the range of about 20 to 80 to 1, depending on the reactor design, which means that the ratio of thorium to ^{238}U is anywhere from 3 to 1 to more than 10 to 1.

The ratios of thorium to ^{233}U and to ^{238}U can vary considerably depending on the type of reactor or on the distribution of fuel in the fertile material within a particular reactor. This is because the relative rate at which neutrons are captured by ^{232}Th and ^{238}U depends strongly on the energy of the neutrons. In turn, the neutron energy at which capture predominantly takes place can depend on the type of neutron moderator and fuel–fertile material distribution in the fuel. At very low neutron energies typical of light-water reactors, the probability of neutron capture in ^{232}Th is about three times as high as it is in ^{238}U. At higher neutron energies (in what is called the *resonance absorption region*), this situation can reverse and the neutron capture probability per atom of ^{238}U can be substantially higher than in ^{232}Th. The latter situation is typical for reactors in which the moderator (the material that slows down neutrons to make them more effective in causing fissions) is graphite instead of water, as in the HTGR. Since the relative concentrations of ^{233}U, ^{238}U, ^{232}Th, and any other materials (such as light water) that capture neutrons must be adjusted to sustain a fission chain reaction in the reactor core, the allowable concentrations of the isotopes can therefore depend strongly on the reactor design.

In any case, the national power plants of our models fueled with a mixture of ^{233}U, ^{238}U, and ^{232}Th will produce both the plutonium isotope, ^{239}Pu, and ^{233}U by neutron capture in ^{238}U or ^{232}Th, respectively. Multiple neutron captures in ^{239}Pu will produce, generally in decreasing amounts, other plutonium isotopes, ^{240}Pu, ^{241}Pu, and ^{242}Pu. Other reactions will produce some ^{238}Pu. These isotopes of plutonium vary considerably in the extent to which they make for good reactor "fuel." For example, ^{239}Pu is *much* better than ^{240}Pu, from this point of view, in the light-water and heavy-water reactors of the types now being used. ^{239}Pu is also substantially better in a plutonium fast breeder reactor. ^{238}Pu and ^{241}Pu are also about as good as ^{239}Pu in current types of power reactors. Analogous considerations apply to other isotopes of uranium produced by neutron capture in ^{233}U. To simplify matters, reactor engineers often use the label *fissile* plutonium to distinguish those plutonium isotopes that make for good fuel, in spite of the fact that under some circumstances, all plutonium isotopes can sustain a chain reaction (as in a nuclear explosive) all by themselves and do in fact fission significantly in some types of power reactors.

We point all this out because the figure of merit in the entire cycle we are most concerned with, the ratio of national to regional power than can be sustained, depends critically on the assumed rate at which consumed fuel is replaced by new fuel, especially as this ratio gets close to 1 for replacement of a consumed atom of ^{233}U or plutonium by an atom of ^{233}U. If that ratio were equal to 1 in the national reactors, the net plutonium left in their spent fuel would not have to be fissioned at all to keep the cycle self-sustaining. In this case, excess plutonium could be converted to ^{233}U in a regional plant, thereby providing additional ^{233}U to help start up national reactors that are part of a new or growing system.

If this conversion ratio drops below 1, then regional reactors are *necessary* to convert the plutonium in the spent fuel of the national reactors to ^{233}U for recycle in order to keep the overall cycle self-sustaining. How much power is required at the regional centers for this purpose depends on a rather large number of key parameters, none of which are easy to estimate without use of complex computer programs and all of which depend importantly on the types of regional and national reactors and on the specific distribution of key isotopes in the fuel of all reactors. Some of these key parameters are listed below, not necessarily in order of importance:

National Reactors

1. Overall conversion ratio (fissile atoms produced per fissile atom consumed)

2. Conversion ratio with respect to production of fissile uranium

3. Conversion ratio with respect to production of fissile plutonium

4. Total power produced per unit weight of fuel between insertion to reactor use and removal as spent fuel

5. Fissile uranium, fissile plutonium, total uranium, and total plutonium per unit weight of fuel in spent fuel

6. Deficit of ^{233}U per unit power produced by national reactors that must be made up by ^{233}U production in regional reactors to make the entire national reactor system self-sustaining

Regional Reactors

1. Overall breeding or conversion ratio

2. Net ^{233}U in spent fuel, per unit mass of plutonium loaded into fresh fuel

Transition to the Thorium Fuel Cycle

We have so far described only a simplified model of a mature thorium fuel cycle system, that is, one that has become self-sustaining and in which the combination of regional facilities and national reactors is no longer expanding its power-generating capacity. But what might happen between now and the time when such nuclear power systems might exist?

We would not expect that a shift to the thorium cycle would start on a substantial scale for at least a decade, even if detailed analyses and engineering tests of major components had by then indicated that this fission alternative should be adopted. During this decade or so, large stockpiles of plutonium produced in reactors based on the once-through fuel cycle would most likely accumulate in repositories for spent reactor fuel. By 1985 this cumulative amount of plutonium could be more than 500,000 kilograms. If this plutonium, along with that produced in reactors that have shifted to the denatured uranium–thorium cycle, were then reprocessed in several regional reprocessing plants, their total capacity should be such that the rate of ^{233}U conversion of the plutonium in regional reactors would roughly equal the demand for supplemental ^{233}U for national reactors already operating on the new fuel cycle and for ^{233}U for reactor cores for new power plants then being built. This demand for ^{233}U will depend strongly on the conversion ratios of the national power plants and on the rate of construction of new plants.

Depending on the timing of a shift to a thorium cycle and the rate of growth of nuclear power, the regional reactors that convert plutonium to ^{233}U may or may not have to be true breeders (i.e., reactors producing more fuel than they consume) during the early stages of the transition. The reason for this is that the amount of plutonium stockpiled by the time the conversion to the new cycle starts in earnest may be sufficient to keep all the national reactors supplied with the supplemental ^{233}U they would require for a decade, or perhaps much longer, even if the regional reactors produce less ^{233}U than they consume in plutonium. Analysis of this possibility would be an important part of the assessment of the thorium-fuel-cycle alternative, especially if one assumes relatively low rates of growth of nuclear power and high conversion ratios for the national power reactors.

FIVE

Conclusion

.

The three fission futures discussed above have radically different security and safeguards implications. Choosing among the three cannot be done rationally until these implications and other relevant factors have been thoroughly explored. It is, after all, the long-term future of nuclear power—when it has achieved a stable maturity—that we ought to have our eye on. It would be foolhardy to foreclose possible attractive future paths by decisions dominated by very short-term concerns of economics and resource management, especially if these immediate concerns are, upon reflection, found uncompelling. There are no compelling advantages to a hastened introduction of a plutonium economy, with its reprocessing and recycling of plutonium; and there is enough time and enough reason to explore the alternatives sketched above. Neither the economic and resource advantages of recycling plutonum in light-water reactors nor the prospect of an early wide-scale introduction of plutonium breeder reactors appears to us sufficiently promising to eclipse the security and safeguards issues we have been concerned with in this paper.

TIME TO THINK

Economics of Recycle   The economic prospects of plutonium recycle in light-water reactors seem especially bleak given the high and apparently still accelerating projected costs of reprocessing. Even were this not so, recycle under most plausible conditions could not be expected to reduce total generating costs by more than a few percent, since fuel-cycle costs represent such a relatively small fraction (about 20 percent) of the total generating costs of nuclear power.

Resource Conservation   Similarly, the savings in uranium resources promised by plutonium recycle in light-water reactors while far from negligible do not appear marked. In equilibrium, with no net increase in reactors in the overall system, recycle of both the uranium and plutonium from the reactor spent fuel could perhaps replace 30 to 40 percent of the uranium (and enrichment) that would otherwise be required. Thus recycle at equilibrium could extend uranium resources by as much as 40 percent, but in this no-growth case there would, by the same token, be no significant pressure on worldwide uranium resources. In a growing system, with the continued necessity of fueling new reactors, the overall savings provided by recycling would be less— perhaps 10 to 20 percent depending upon the growth rate projections. The amount of available high-grade uranium resources could become a serious issue in the case of a growing system, but recycle would extend the uranium resource base by only 10 to 20 percent. The faster the growth rate of nuclear power, the less significant will be the recycle savings.

Prelude to the Breeder   Whereas recycle in light-water reactors can extend uranium resources only marginally, the plutonium breeder reactors can do so dramatically. The breeder system could potentially increase the amount of natural uranium that can be ultimately fissioned in a reactor by a factor of about 100; and whereas reprocessing spent fuel is not necessary for a system of light-water (or other converter) reactors, it is of course central to a breeding cycle.

However, the case for breeders—the value and timing of their introduction—is very sensitive to the question of how quickly high-grade uranium reserves available on the world market will be used up by ordinary reactors. This rate of exhaustion of uranium, we believe, may be considerably less than hitherto thought. In every industrialized country whose nuclear programs we are familiar with (including the United States, France, Germany, Japan, and the United Kingdom), plans for the development of nuclear power have recently been substantially scaled down. Taking the industrialized noncommunist countries as a whole, it now seems unlikely that nuclear power growth will outstrip available high-grade uranium reserves for a very long while, probably not before the year 2000.

In the long run, of course, high-grade uranium resources will run out and countries may be compelled to operate plutonium breeders, insofar as fission power is to have a sustained, important role in energy production. But even if this is so, such decisions can safely be left to the future. Whatever the growth rate of nuclear power and its claim on uranium reserves, it appears doubtful that any country (France possibly excepted) will be in a position to deploy breeders widely on a commercial scale before the late 1980s or even later. As a consequence, the amounts of plutonium that will be needed to fuel the first breeders will probably not be very large for at least a decade and a half or longer. There seems no reason to separate plutonium *now* for possible use in breeder reactors 15 to 20 years hence. This is all the more so if it is recognized that plutonium breeders may *never* be deployed.

There is, in sum, time to wait, look, listen, and think before we commit ourselves to a specific nuclear future. What ought to be done while we are waiting is embodied in our previous discussion. First, it is important to invent and explore nuclear futures that are as diversion-proof as possible, with safeguards considerations predominating the choice of nuclear technology rather than simply grafted onto technologies after the fact. From our discussion in Chapter 4 of one such possible nuclear future, based on a thorium breeding cycle, it is evident that the research agendas associated with such investigation could be very rich and engaging indeed.

It is above all imperative, in the time we give ourselves before embarking on one nuclear path or another, that the possible nonfossil alternatives to nuclear power be carefully studied. This is especially true for solar energy, which in a variety of forms is at present being inventively investigated by groups all over the world. The prospects are excellent that solar energy can be developed and implemented on a large scale in a period of time comparable to that required to develop fully safeguarded breeder systems.

These arguments are somewhat speculative and preliminary, and our optimism (if that is the word) concerning nuclear-electric growth and solar energy prospects may ultimately prove to be ill founded. If so, there will not be as strong an argument against plutonium breeders as we now think or as much time to choose our energy future as we now hope.

But there is, in any event, time to see whether low nuclear-electric and high solar projections are in fact reasonable. During this period, it appears especially important that we do not stumble onto the plutonium path and foreclose the alternatives.

TIME TO ACT

The worldwide development of the nuclear industry has not yet been seriously affected by security and safeguards considerations. The basic reactor technologies and fuel-cycle configurations that promise to dominate the industry in the future have been contrived with virtually no significant prior weight given to their impact on the risks of proliferation and criminal diversion. Safeguards will have to be applied in a scrambling and haphazard fashion to technologies propelled by factors having nothing to do with international security. The technologies of the plutonium economy are cases in point. The recycle of plutonium in light-water reactors and eventually in fast breeders will require safeguards of a most complex and cumbersome sort at best; at worst, the international community will not even be able to muster the will and energy to emplace effective safeguards at all. Currently there is no clearly understood way effectively to safeguard the plutonium economy.

It is time to place safeguards at the forefront of our thinking and to inquire whether it is possible to shape a nuclear fuel cycle that is consistent with the principles of effective safeguards, instead of letting the technology develop first with safeguards then tagging along. We have looked at two such possibilities above—one the drastically simple alternative of a long-term complete phase-out of nuclear fission; and the other a breeding cycle founded upon thorium as the principal fertile material and denatured ^{233}U as the fuel of commerce at national reactors.

Each of these long-term paths for the development of nuclear power could go far toward providing a technical fix to the danger of criminal or terrorist diversion of weapons-grade material from civilian power programs. Each also promises a marked, though limited, discouragement of latent proliferation by forcing a sharp distinction between civilian nuclear power and national nuclear weapons programs.

Each of the alternatives does have difficult features, however. A long-term dependence on a once-through fuel cycle will probably require an eventual dramatic expansion of the use of solar energy, a development that would certainly involve substantial technological and institutional innovation. The international thorium-cycle path would also require technical innovation and, as well, an unprecedented expansion of international institutions. The system we have outlined resembles the modified version of the Baruch plan for the international control of nuclear energy that the United States submitted to the United Nations in 1946. Unlike that plan, our scheme permits the national development, deployment, and control of nuclear reactors (and, in the countries that now have them, nuclear weapons as well!); but it does in effect require international control of all other parts of the nuclear fuel cycle in the long run.

We do not believe that these difficulties and "impracticalities" are insurmountable or that they should deter further study. As we have insisted in this study, *any* energy future that we choose will be difficult and painful. The plutonium economy is consistent with current industry plans and therefore may seem less impractical than the alternatives, but a systematic and effective safeguarding of plutonium will involve, as fully as will any of the other future fission paths, a complex set of institutional arrangements. The deceptive ease of a slide into a plutonium economy should not fool us into narrow vision. The energy future is much richer in possibilities than we have yet fully realized. Our main objective in this study has been to insist that the involved countries carefully explore at least some of these possibilities before plunging down one path or another.

For this reason, we have urged as our lone specific near-term policy recommendation that plutonium not be separated from spent fuel from civilian reactors anywhere in the world until alternatives to plutonium recycling have been thoroughly assessed.

This recommendation, and indeed our entire argument, is addressed to every concerned country. We believe that the search for a strategy to minimize the risks of criminal and terrorist diversion and to impede latent proliferation is ultimately in the interests of the entire international community and should not be thought of as the goal of only a few privileged countries. This does not mean, however, that all countries have to act in concert at once. Each country will first want to get its own house in order, an endeavor that will send strong signals to other

189

countries. There is a place in an equitable nonproliferation strategy for countries foregoing reprocessing and other activities within their own borders to refuse to export them to others. Thus we would hope that persons who otherwise respect our arguments do not argue nevertheless that their countries should not accept our conclusions simply because some other countries may not cooperate.

We are finally uneasy that we may be misunderstood because of the special focus we have adopted in this study. There are two points in particular that we wish to insist upon. First, we do not think that there is any technical fix, much less a simple one, to prevent nuclear proliferation. A nonproliferation strategy that does not grapple with the political and security incentives for countries to acquire nuclear weapons and the political constraints to doing so cannot hope to succeed. One cannot wave the magic wand of a thorium cycle or some other technical innovation to make an essentially political problem turn into a technical one. Still more fundamentally, we do not believe that in the long term proliferation can be significantly impeded while one class of countries (the nuclear weapons states) acts as if nuclear weapons are politically useful and insists on the special privilege of possessing them while denying the weapons to others.

EDITOR'S NOTE: Messrs. Taylor and Feiveson are continuing their study of the issues raised in this essay. It is likely that the results of their further work will be published by the 1980s Project.

Glossary

NUCLEAR MATERIALS

^{238}U—the isotope of uranium that exists in a concentration of over 99 percent in natural uranium and is not suitable for nuclear explosives.

^{235}U—the isotope of uranium found at a concentration of about 0.7 percent in natural uranium. This concentration of ^{235}U must be increased (through "enrichment") to about 3 percent for use as fuel in United States reactors, and to a higher concentration, normally about 90 percent, for nuclear explosives. As the concentration of ^{235}U increases, the amount required for an explosive (i.e., the "critical mass") decreases.

^{233}U—an isotope of uranium that does not exist in nature in significant amounts. It is produced in reactors that contain thorium, and it is suitable for use in making nuclear explosives.

Plutonium—an element not found in nature but which is produced in reactors by the transformation of ^{238}U fuel. The isotope of plutonium produced in greatest abundance is ^{239}Pu, though ^{240}Pu and ^{241}Pu may also be present in plutonium material. Plutonium is suitable for use in making nuclear explosives, in which case the higher the concentration of ^{239}Pu the "better."

Thorium—an element whose isotope, ^{232}Th, exists in nature and can be used, generally speaking, as a substitute for ^{238}U in nuclear power cycles. The use of thorium in reactor fuel yields ^{233}U (the use of uranium yields plutonium) which can be used in nuclear explosives.

NUCLEAR FACILITIES AND EQUIPMENT

Light-water reactor (LWR)—the most common type of power reactor, fueled by uranium that must be partially enriched (from 2 to 4 percent ^{235}U) above its natural isotopic composition. The spent fuel of an LWR contains significant amounts of plutonium, which could, after some further processing, be used to make nuclear explosives.

CANDU reactor (or, more generally, heavy-water reactor—HWR)— power reactor that is fueled by natural uranium and uses heavy water to slow down neutrons. The commercial development of this reactor has been pursued primarily by Canada (thus the name CANDU). The spent fuel of a CANDU reactor contains significant amounts of plutonium, which could, after some processing, be used to make nuclear explosives.

High-temperature gas-cooled reactor (HTGR)—a reactor type, not widely used for power generation, that uses as fuel highly enriched (90–95 percent) uranium, which could, after some processing, also be used to make nuclear explosives. The spent fuel of an HTGR does not contain significant amounts of plutonium, but does contain ^{233}U that could be used for explosives.

"Breeder" reactor (or liquid metal fast breeder reactor)—a reactor now under intensive development that would produce more nuclear fuel than it consumes while generating power. "Breeding" of fuel in a reactor occurs when more free neutrons are being absorbed in ^{238}U (thus producing plutonium, which can subsequently be used as fuel) than are needed to sustain fission for the release of energy. This capacity to "breed" fuel would dramatically extend the life expectancy of natural uranium reserves. A breeder reactor would discharge annually seven times as much plutonium as an LWR of comparable power capacity. (Breeder technology is most commonly identified with the ^{238}U plutonium cycle but may also be applicable to a thorium ^{233}U cycle.)

Enrichment plant—a facility required to increase the ratio of ^{235}U to ^{238}U above that found in natural uranium, which is about 0.7 percent ^{235}U to 99.3 percent ^{238}U. Altering the isotopic composition of any given element cannot be done by chemical processes, requiring instead what has been historically a far more difficult and costly process called "enrichment" or "isotopic separation." The two principal types of enrichment plants are the gaseous diffusion and gas centrifuge types. Uranium must be enriched for use in LWRs, HTGRs, and nuclear explosives.

Reprocessing plant—a facility required to separate the elements present in spent reactor fuel. The plutonium recovered through reprocessing can be reused as reactor fuel or for nuclear explosives.

TERMS

Safeguards—the various procedures designed to deter the diversion of materials from civilian nuclear power activities for possible use in explosives.

Fission—the process whereby atomic nuclei are split apart as a result of bombardment by neutrons, yielding vast amounts of energy as well as more neutrons capable of causing further fission.

Recycle—the reuse of spent reactor fuel material for fresh reactor fuel, following chemical reprocessing to separate the various elements found in spent fuel. The recycle technology being developed today makes use of the plutonium produced in LWRs and CANDU reactors for fresh reactor fuel. This plutonium can also be used in nuclear explosives.

Selected Bibliography

Blood, Archer K., "Nuclear Proliferation and the Indian Explosion," *Parameters,* vol. 5, no. 1 (1975), pp. 46–50.

Chayes, Abram, and W. Bennett Lewis (eds.)., *International Arrangements for Nuclear Fuel Cycle Facilities,* Ballinger Publishing Co., Cambridge, Mass, 1976.

Dunn, Lewis A., and Herman Kahn, *Trends in Nuclear Proliferation, 1975–1995,* HI-2336-RR, Hudson Institute, Croton-on-Hudson, N.Y., October 15, 1975.

Epstein, William, *The Last Chance: Nuclear Proliferation and Arms Control,* The Free Press, New York, 1976.

Greenwood, Ted, George W. Rathjens, and Jack Ruina, *Nuclear Power Technology and Nuclear Weapons Proliferation,* Adelphi Paper No. 131, International Institute for Strategic Studies, London, 1976.

Krieger, David, "Terrorists and Nuclear Technology," *Bulletin of the Atomic Scientists,* June 1975, pp. 28–34.

Leachman, Robert B., and Phillip Althoff (eds.), *Preventing Nuclear Theft: Guidelines for Industry and Government,* Praeger Publications, New York, 1972.

Marks, Anne W. (ed.), *NPT: Paradoxes and Problems,* Arms Control Association, Carnegie Endowment for International Peace, Washington, D.C., 1975.

Marwah, Onkar, and Ann Schulz (eds.), *Nuclear Proliferation and the Near-Nuclear Countries,* Ballinger Publishing Co., Cambridge, Mass., 1975.

McPhee, John, *The Curve of Binding Energy,* Farrar, Straus & Giroux, Inc., New York, 1974.

Quester, George, *The Politics of Nuclear Proliferation,* The Johns Hopkins University Press, Baltimore, 1973.

Scheinmann, Lawrence, *Atomic Energy in France under the Fourth Republic,* Princeton University Press, Princeton, N.J., 1965.

Schoettle, Enid Curtis Bok, *Long-term Arms Limitations and Security Requirements for Minimizing the Proliferation of Nuclear Weapons,* Stockholm International Peace Research Institute Monograph Series, forthcoming.

Ullman, Richard, "No First Use of Nuclear Weapons," *Foreign Affairs,* vol. 50, no. 4 (July 1972), pp. 669–683.

Von Hipple, Frank, and Robert H. Williams, "Energy Waste and Nuclear Power Growth," *Bulletin of the Atomic Scientists,* December 1976.

Willrich, Mason (ed.), *International Safeguards and Nuclear Industry,* The Johns Hopkins University Press, Baltimore, 1973.

————, and Theodore B. Taylor, *Nuclear Theft: Risks and Safeguards,* Ballinger Publishing Co., Cambridge, Mass., 1974.

Wohlstetter, Albert, Thomas A. Brown, Gregory Jones, David McGarvey, Henrey Rowen, Vincent Taylor, and Roberta Wohlstetter, *Moving toward Life in a Nuclear Armed Crowd?* ACDA/PAB 263 and PH76-04-384-14, Pan Heuristics, Los Angeles, 1976.

Wohlstetter, Roberta, "Terror on a Grand Scale," *Survival,* vol. XVIII, no. 3, May/ June 1976, pp. 98–104.

Index

threats of Russian intervention in,
116–117
Ecology:
coal and, 127
geothermal energy and, 127
nuclear power and, 2
solar energy and, 128
waste management and, 91
Egypt, 121
Non-Proliferation Treaty and, 152
Israel and, 77
regional security interests of, 163
Russian nuclear arms to, possibility of, 76
U.S. security guarantees and, 58
England, 16
breeder reactor program in, 129, 152
export agreements and, 171
NATO alliance and, 57
as nuclear power, 50
nuclear umbrella of, 47
plans for nuclear power in, 186
reactor industry of, 87
restrictions on, 170
reprocessing fuel in, 128, 151
safeguards and security agreement of, 87
sanctions against India, 53
Eritrean Liberation Front, 99
Exxon Corporation, 151
Exxon Nuclear, 146

France, 121
bilateral agreements of, 154
breeder reactor program in, 129, 152, 186
as exporter: export agreements, 171, 173
of fuel reprocessors, 3, 8, 92
of package deals, 88, 92
of reactors, 87, 126
reducing incentives, 93
NATO alliance and, 57
Non-Proliferation Treaty and, 78
as nuclear power, 50
origin of, 55
nuclear umbrella of, 47
plans for nuclear power in, 186

rejection of nuclear weapons agreements,
10
reprocessing technology of, 88, 128, 151
restrictions of nuclear power and, 170, 173
safeguards and security agreement of, 87
United States nuclear policy's effect on, 10
Frye, Alton, 75

Geothermal energy, 127–128
Glossary, 191–193
Great Britain (see England)
Guerrillas (see Non-state entities)

Hiroshima, 26, 27, 137
Hungary, 47

India, 13n., 16, 70, 120
avowed peaceful nuclear detonation, 31,
37, 67, 81
United States acceptance of, 68
economic assistance after nuclear
explosion, 51
erosion of Third World leadership role, 52
as exporter of fuel reprocessors, 92
fostering sense of nuclear inevitability, 111
future test program of, 72
hints at nuclear capability, 72
Non-Proliferation Treaty and, 78, 152,
157
reactor industry of, 87, 151
regional security of, 41, 46, 47, 163
reprocessing fuel in, 128, 151
restrictions on nuclear power and, 170
Russia and, 76
sanctions against, 53
secret decision by few to go nuclear, 56
sequential steps of nuclearization and, 148
Indian Ocean Zone of Peace, 64
Indonesia, 15, 120
leverage against going nuclear, 77
nuclear competition and, 40
Oceania nuclear-free-zone and, 65

204

testing of, 31, 43
  banning, 116
  disguised at PNEs, 68
  by non-state entities, 99
  rate of, 34
threatened use of, 26, 27
unique context of decision to use, 35
United States withdrawal of foreign
  placed, 2
unplanned use of, 26–28, 40
uranium enrichment technology for, 5, 6,
  32–34
wealth and, 16
(*See also* Conventional weapons;
  Disincentives to acquiring nuclear
  weapons)

Oceania nuclear-free-zone, 64, 65, 113
Once-through fuel cycle, 126–127
  civilian nuclear diversion and, 147
  full power potential of, 140
  safeguards against plutonium theft and,
    139, 140, 160–161, 182, 189
OPEC (Organization of Petroleum
  Exporting Countries):
  aid to Third World, 73
  boycott of 1973, 81
  effect on United States nuclear policy of,
    10
  price increase by, 18*n.*
Organization for Economic Cooperation and
  Development, redistribution of global
  wealth and, 73

Pakistan, 13*n.,* 15, 17, 121
  bilateral agreements of, 154
  conventional arms for, 61
  credibility of United States alliance with,
    59
  effect on United States nuclear policy of,
    10
  Non-Proliferation Treaty and, 152
  nuclear competition and, 40
  nuclear program in, 170, 171
  regional security of, 46, 163

reprocessing fuel in, 129, 151
restrictions on nuclear power and, 173
security concerns and nuclear guarantees,
  11, 42
United States guarantees and not going
  nuclear, 76–77, 93
Palestinian Liberation Organization, 99
Partial Test Ban Treaty, 54
Peaceful nuclear explosives (PNEs), 31,
  67–68, 114
Petroleum:
  curbing nuclear proliferation and, 2
  eroded confidence in supplies of, 81
  price rise in, 18*n.,* 54
Philippine Islands, 65, 170
Plutonium, 128–130
  anticipated costs of, 84
  CANDU reactors and, 88–89
  chemical reprocessing of, 140, 145
  crude nuclear weapons and, 136–137
  decreased reliance on, 8
  disposal of, 160
  explosive device and, 34
  isotopes of, 136, 137, 145
  large-scale use of, 152
  liquid-metal assembly technology, 129
  once-through fuel cycle and, 126–127
    safeguards against theft in, 139, 140,
      160–161, 182, 189
  oxide, 137
  production by country, 142–143
  production reactors, 145
  quantities of, 138–139
  recycle/breeder programs, 8, 85,
    128–131, 140–141, 150, 174,’187, 188
    economics of, 185–186
  reducing dangers of recycling, 90–91
  regenerative properties of, 2
  reprocessing for weapons of, 5, 7, 32–34,
    54, 132, 144–146, 160, 164, 175
    new developments in, 33
  shielding of, 140
  shipping of, 91
  simplified method of obtaining, 33, 86
  in spent fuel, 126
  stockpiling of, 91, 126, 164, 174, 175,
    182, 183

civilian nuclear power diversion, 146–147
conventional arms support by the United
 States, 61
enrichment: facilities in, 90
 technology in, 86
as exporter of fuel reprocessors, 92
as high-risk nuclear state, 28
as isolated state, 42, 163
leverage against going nuclear, 77, 93
Non-Proliferation Treaty and, 152, 157
nuclear industry in, 72, 151
regional security interests of, 17, 38
 United States and, 72
relations with United States, 58–59
sanctions against, 53
U.S.S.R. (*see* Soviet Union)
United Reprocessors, 91, 151
United States:
 Baruch plan, 189
 bilateral agreements of, 153, 154
 breeder reactor technology in, 88, 129, 152
 a competing spheres of influence world
  and, 60
 conflict with allies over reprocessing fuel, 3
 conflicts in foreign policy of, 113
 Congress, 53
 credibility of, 2, 59, 63
  "abandoned" states going nuclear and,
   112–113
  down-play of weapons and, 70
  increase in, 60
  no-first-use policy and, 68–69
  pressuring allies and, 93
 and Cuban extradition agreement, 102
 declining enthusiasm for PNEs in, 67
 evolution of strategic balance and, 12–15
 export agreements and, 171, 173
 future international involvement of, 59–60
 global security interests and, 38, 72
  Middle East settlements and, 58
 India's weapons intentions and, 68
 joint action against proliferation by Russia
  and, 74, 75, 114
 light-water reactors and, 126
 limits to unilateral action by, 10
 military-industrial-nuclear-research
  complex, 9–10

no-first-use policy, 68–69
no-use-against-non-nuclear-states
 declaration, 63, 116
non-state entity nuclear use against, 102
nuclear-free-zones and, 64
Nuclear Fuel Service plant, 151
nuclear guarantees to threatened states, 11,
 41
 England and France going nuclear and,
  57
 retrenching of, 59
nuclear protection against, 44–46
nuclear threats against, 106
nuclear umbrella of, 2, 47
economic interests and, 50
extending, 58–59, 113
perpetuation of dependency via, 12
security treaties and, 57–60, 112
weakening of, 42–43, 45
plans for nuclear power in, 186
plutonium theft by criminals and, 136
pressuring allies against going nuclear,
 76–77, 93
proliferation, and security policies of, 8
protection against Chinese blackmail,
 61–62
public pronouncements concerning
 weapons, 69–70, 116
reactor market: control of, 87
 new technology in, 89
 uncertainities in, 89
relations with South Africa, 58–59, 120
reprocessing plant in, 91, 128, 151, 166
restrictions on nuclear power and, 170, 171
safeguards and security agreement of, 87
 failure to encourage others to abide by,
  88
sale of reactors to Iran, 151–152
sanctions against proliferation, 53
secretive wartime decision to go nuclear,
 55
South Korea and, 119
stockpiling of uranium and, 90
supplying nuclear weapons to an ally, 113
Taiwan and, 119
targeting nuclear weapons facilities, 75
technology denial and, 171

About the Authors

TED GREENWOOD is assistant professor of political science at the Massachusetts Institute of Technology and research associate of the Program for Science and International Affairs at Harvard University. He received a B.S. in mathematics and physics from the University of Toronto in 1967, an M.S. in physics from M.I.T. in 1970, and a Ph.D. in political science from M.I.T. in 1973. He is the author of *Making the MIRV: A Study of Nuclear Defense Decision Making* and articles dealing with strategic intelligence, nuclear strategy, nuclear proliferation, and energy policy.

HAROLD A. FEIVESON is assistant professor of public and international affairs at the Woodrow Wilson School of Princeton University, and a member of Princeton's Center for Environmental Studies. He was formerly a member of the Science Bureau of the U.S. Arms Control and Disarmament Agency. He received his Ph.D. from Princeton University in 1972. He is co-editor of the recently published *Boundaries of Analysis—An Inquiry into the Tocks Dam Controversy.*

THEODORE B. TAYLOR is visiting lecturer in the aerospace and mechanical sciences department of Princeton University. He was Chairman of the Board of International Research and Technology Corporation, Arlington, Virginia, from 1967 to 1976, Deputy Director (scientific) of the Defense Atomic Support Agency from 1964 to 1966, Senior Research Advisor at General Atomic from 1956 to 1964, and staff member of the Theoretical Division of Los Alamos Scientific Laboratory from 1949 to 1956. He received a B.S. in physics from California Institute of Technology and a Ph.D. in theoretical physics from Cornell University in 1954. For his work on nuclear weapons design and the TRIGA research reactor, he was one of the recipients of the Atomic Energy Commission's Ernest O. Lawrence Award in 1965. He is co-author of *The Restoration of the Earth,* and *Nuclear Theft: Risks and Safeguards.*

DAVID C. GOMPERT is a senior fellow of the 1980s Project at the Council on Foreign Relations.